"After years of lecturing beginning film students
about the things I confront every day as a Director of Photography,
I decided to write it down."

C.R.Bell

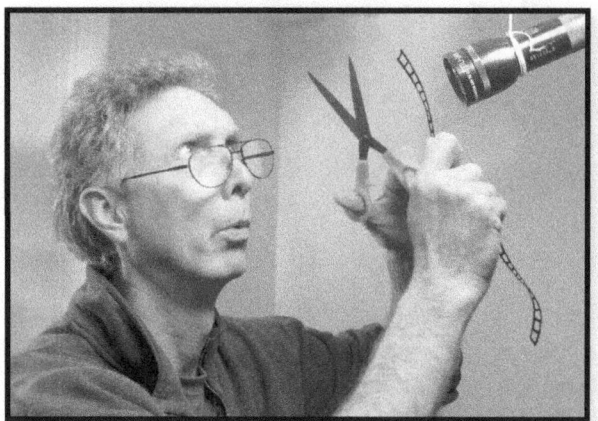

I0461813

Published in 2011 by Bothy Studios LLC, Seattle, WA
www.guerrillafilmguide.com
ISBN: 9780615457000
Book Design, Illustration & Layout: C.R.Bell
Printed by: Lightning Source Inc
www.lightningsource.com

The Guerrilla Guide To Moviemaking

HOW TO MAKE A PROFESSIONAL LOOKING FILM OR VIDEO WHEN YOU HAVE LIMITED RESOURCES

Second Edition   Conceived, Written, and Illustrated by C.R.Bell

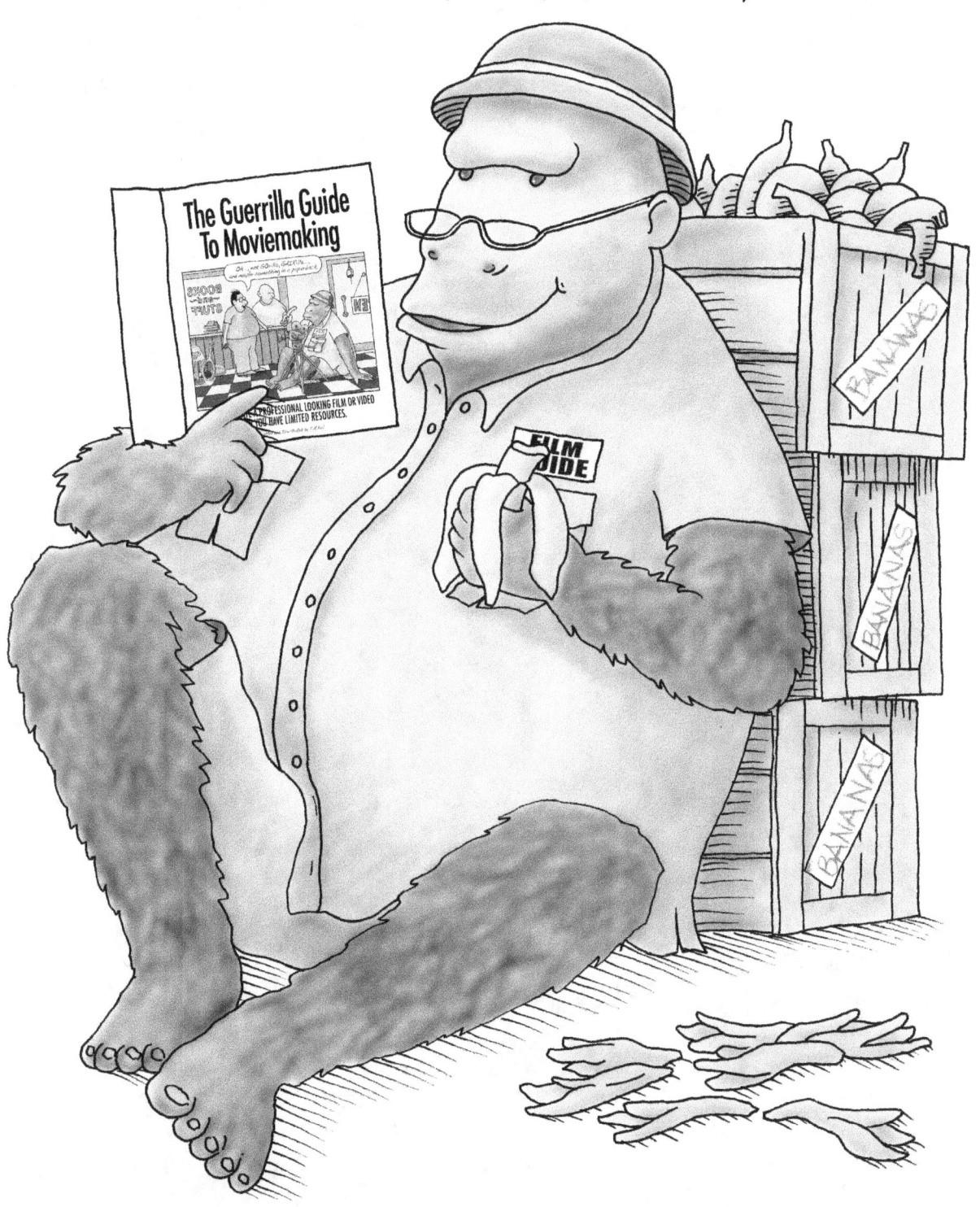

TABLE OF CONTENTS

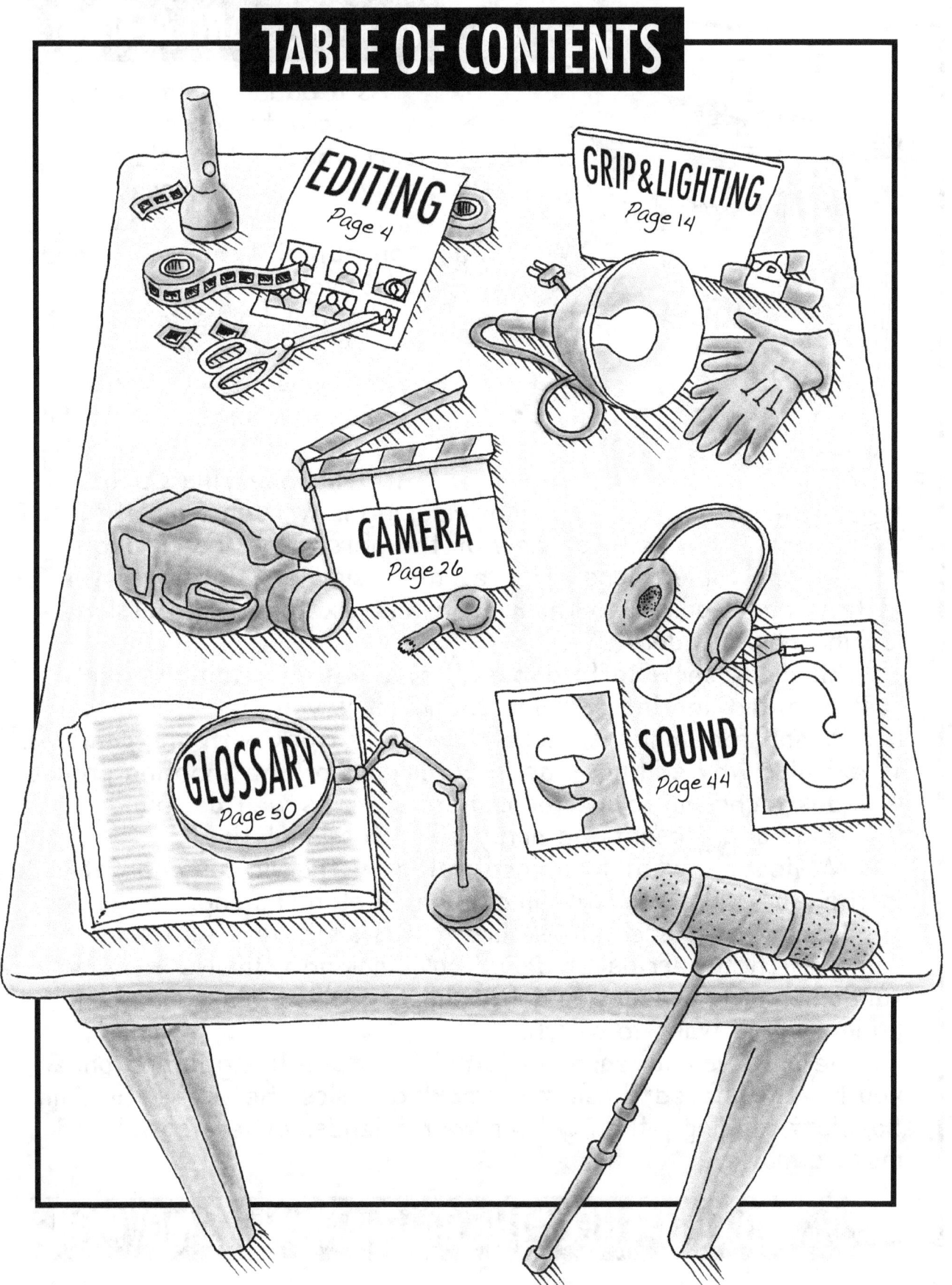

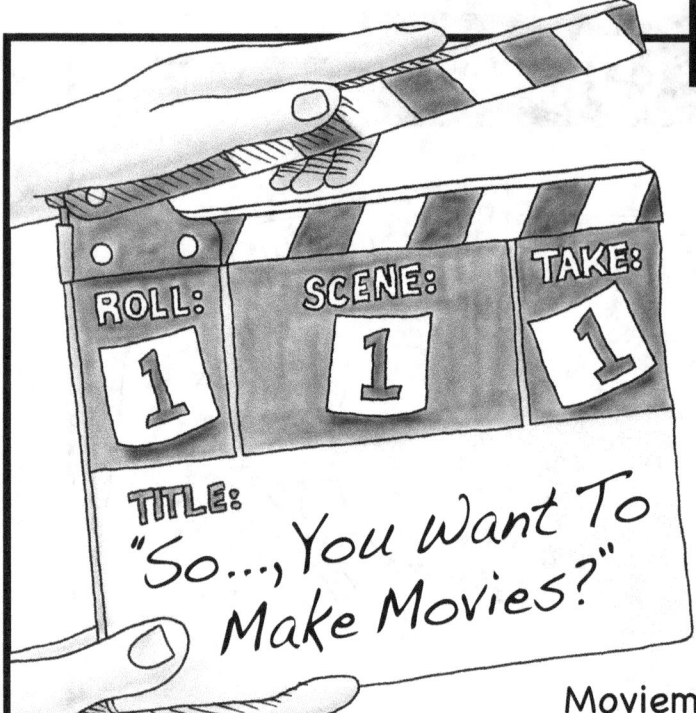

TITLE: "So..., You Want To Make Movies?"

As a budding filmmaker, you owe it to yourself to learn the fundamentals of how to economically produce a visually pleasing, conceptually captivating and creatively clever film.

Lots of books talk about the filmmaking process, but few focus on how to make a film look bigger than the budget available to produce it. The Guerrilla Guide To Moviemaking is written from the point of view of the person looking through the camera lens. It presents a simple overview of the little things required to think about and execute a professional looking film or video.

This guide shows affordable alternatives to traditional high cost grip and lighting equipment, and gives you ideas for how to use it (and the bonus is, these techniques work with any camera). It explains why editing is an integral part of the shooting process, includes technical advice for camera work as well as sound recording and presents an array of professional tips.

Moviegoers want to be captivated by the visuals and get lost in the story—not wish the image would stop shaking, or wonder why every other scene looks like it was shot with a different camera. The Guerrilla Guide To Moviemaking will give you the fundamental knowledge and the simple tools to make films an audience will want to watch.

The only way to learn this craft is by practicing it, and once you have mastered these moviemaking basics the sky is the limit. So, start reading--then gather your friends, write a script and make a movie.

...AND CUT! CHECK THE GATE, AND LET'S MOVE ON

MOVIE MISER'S MANIFESTO

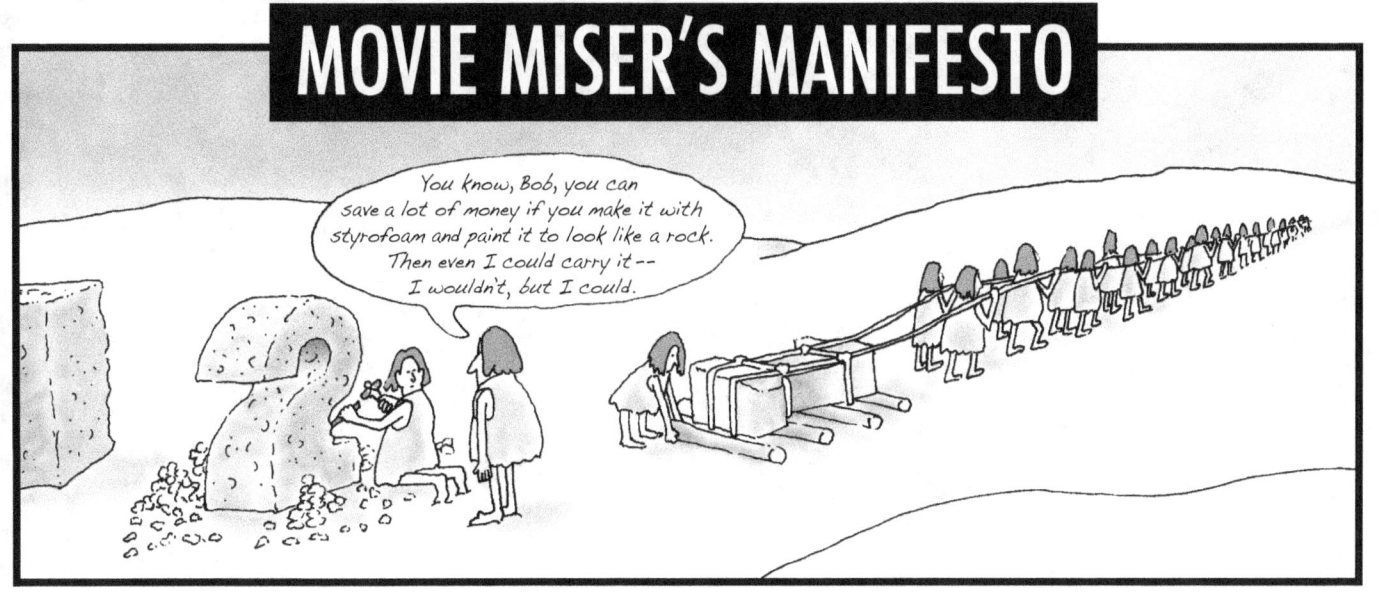

THINK OUTSIDE THE BOX STORE

1. Hardware stores are full of cheap grip and lighting supplies. But don't limit yourself; you may find a useful tool or gadget at a thrift store or an auto parts store. It's amazing what your subconscious mind will see once you start thinking about production.

NEED TO SAVE MONEY? CREATE A FOUNDATION

2. Knowing the basics of how to edit, how to light and how the camera works will save you time and money, as well as give you more confidence during the production process. It will also free your mind to focus more on the big picture.

STAY SMALL TO LOOK BIG

3. With limited resources, the smaller you can work in a scene the more control you will have to make it look great, and the faster you will be able to move. A bigger scene will require more equipment and more time.

DON'T SHOOT THE EDITOR

4. Shooting different angles of the same scene will give you options in editing. All but one angle of the scene may end up on the editing room floor, but if you only shoot one angle and that angle doesn't work, the editor may be the thing that ends up on the editing room floor (crying).

SHOOT FOR THE MIDDLE AND YOU'LL RISE TO THE TOP

5. Creating a phenomenal looking film is much easier when you learn how to shoot a fundamentally sound image that can be color corrected in editing. If you create a look in the camera that can not be changed, you're stuck with it.

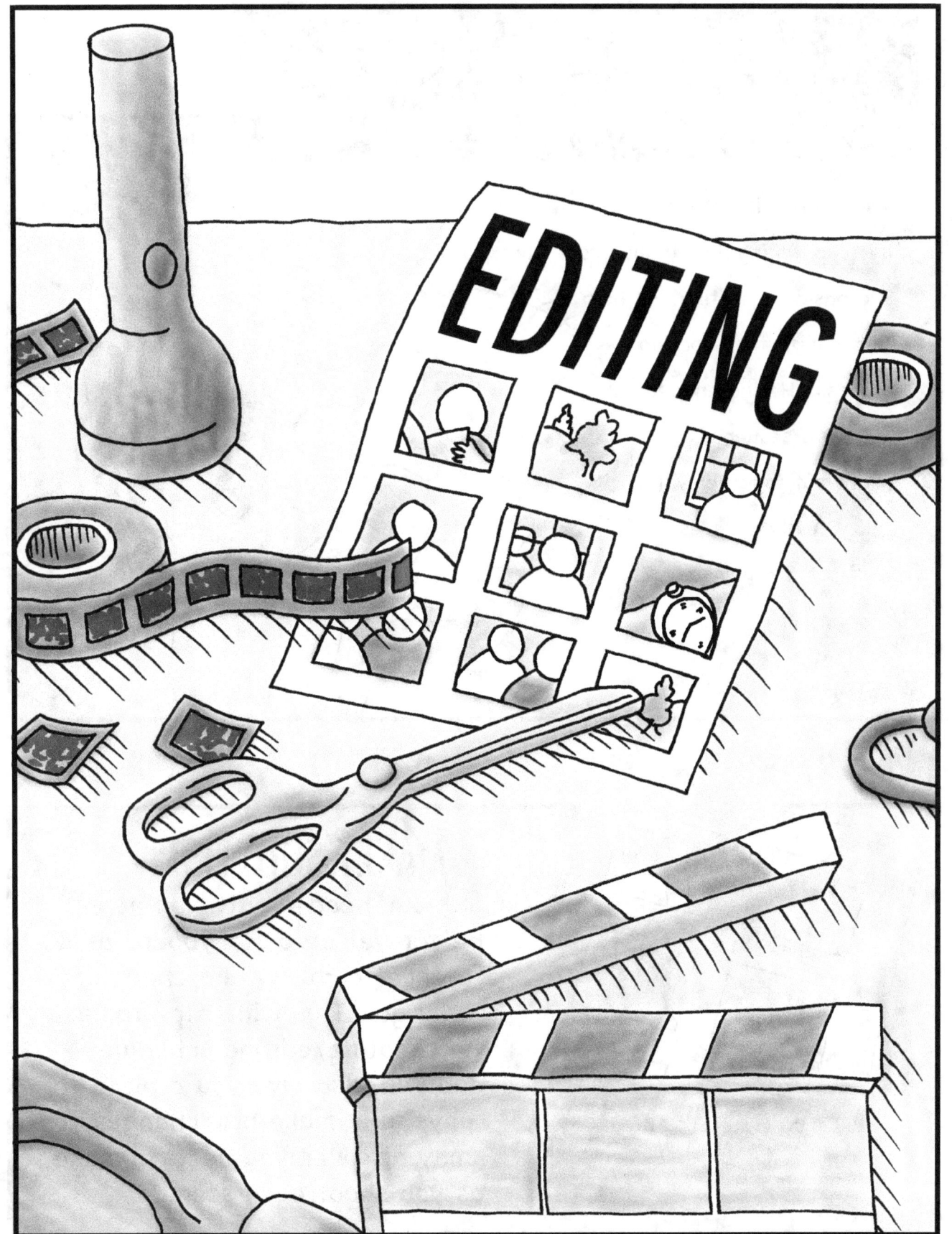

KNOWING HOW TO EDIT WILL TEACH YOU HOW TO SHOOT

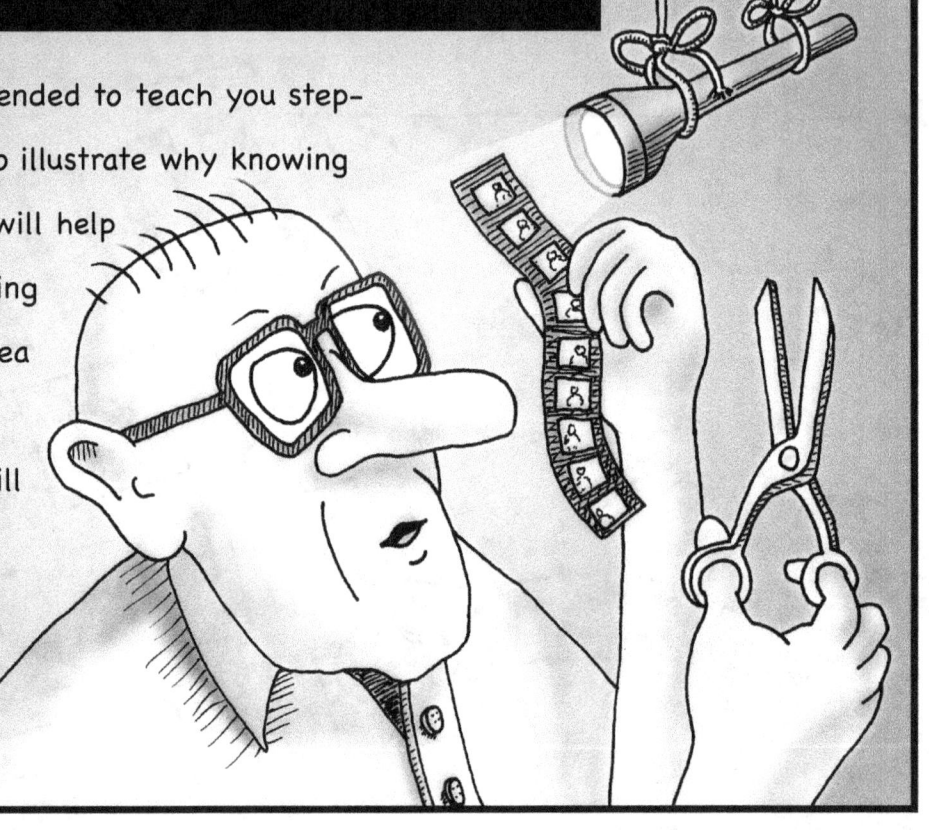

This section is not intended to teach you step-by-step editing, but to illustrate why knowing the basics of editing will help to organize the shooting process. Having an idea of how a sequence might cut together will tell you what scenes to shoot and how to shoot them.

MAKE A SHOT LIST

Not in your head -- put it on paper or better yet on a storyboard as a reference to follow and check off as you go. This will help organize the shooting/editing schedule and will also give you a place to physically make any changes you may discover you need to make as you shoot each scene.

"PHOTOS AT CAMPFIRE"

FIRE CLOSE UP

MED. OF GUY BEHIND FIRE

change angle to low from more in front

WIDE OF GUY-PICKS UP PHOTOS

CLOSE UP THROUGH FIRE

OVER SHOULDER LOOKING AT PHOTOS

EXTREME WIDE WITH SUN SETTING

add closeup of photos

SHOOTING BASIC COVERAGE

Whenever possible cover the scene as a wide master — then move in to get medium coverage, close-up coverage and cutaways.

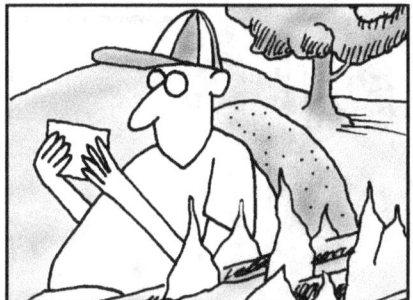
Wide Master

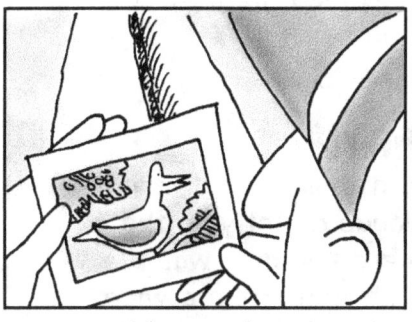
Medium

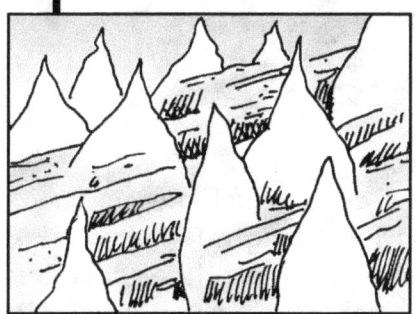

CUTAWAYS

A cutaway can save an edit and/or add tension to a scene. It gives the editor someplace to go if there is a need to cheat a cut or condense a scene. It can also be an interesting way to help tell the story. Keep it relevant and make it interesting--the hands of a clock, a foot tapping or handwringing, a bird flitting in a cage, something that shows emotion or action. Stay away from inanimate objects. Try to find something that has movement.

Cutaway

Close-Up

EDITING SOFTWARE

There are quite a few editing programs out there that are perfectly acceptable for editing. Keeping it simple is the key to most good edits—cuts, dissolves; simple transitions that move the story along without getting in the way. Special effects require a system with a bit more power because they require a lot of rendering. That becomes another discussion, but it is a great advantage to have the ability to manipulate the image with color correction and stylizing effects, which goes hand in hand with a set of scopes -- a waveform monitor for overall exposure levels and a vectorscope for overall color balance.

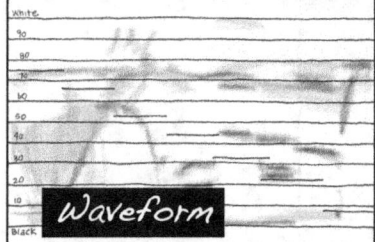
Waveform

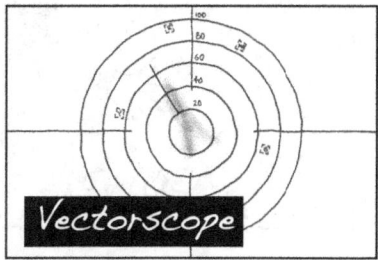
Vectorscope

CUTS

Use cuts for continuous scenes happening in real time.

Use dissolves to depict a lapse of time, moving from one moment to another moment — earlier or later.

DISSOLVES

ANGLES ANGLES ANGLES

Shooting the same scene from different angles will give the editor much more to work with. Changing the focal length (wider or tighter) and moving off the axis in any direction (a rule of thumb is at least 25° to make it appear to be different) will make for a much more interesting cut.

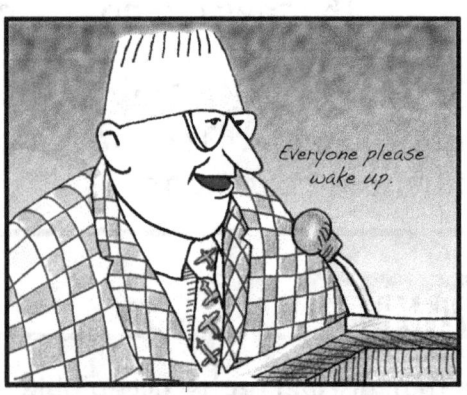

Everyone please wake up.

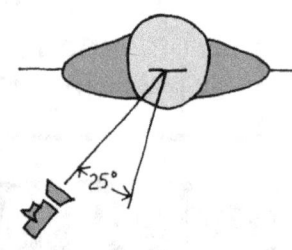

25°

HOWEVER...

When talent is delivering dialogue directly to the camera you may want to cut straight from a wide shot to a tight shot without an angle change to keep the continuity of the eyes looking into the lens.

BUT...

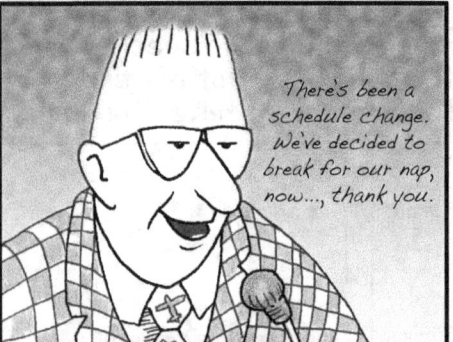

There's been a schedule change. We've decided to break for our nap, now..., thank you.

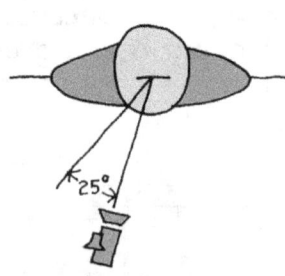

25°

If you do want to change the angle, you can add a head turn, as long as you include the head turn at the end of the scene you are cutting from and at the beginning of the scene you are cutting to.

TRANSITIONS FROM SCENE TO SCENE

Pan or Tilt... Another way to smoothly change the angle is to pan or tilt from something in the scene. Let's say you are shooting a construction site and you need a bunch of scenes of a backhoe digging a hole.

If you start with a scene shooting the action from the front, then cut directly to a scene shooting the action from the side, you will need to match the action of the digging bucket to make the cut work. But, if you add a transition to the next scene with a tilt down from the sky or up from the dirt, you can move into the action at almost any point because the viewer didn't see what happened during the pan or tilt.

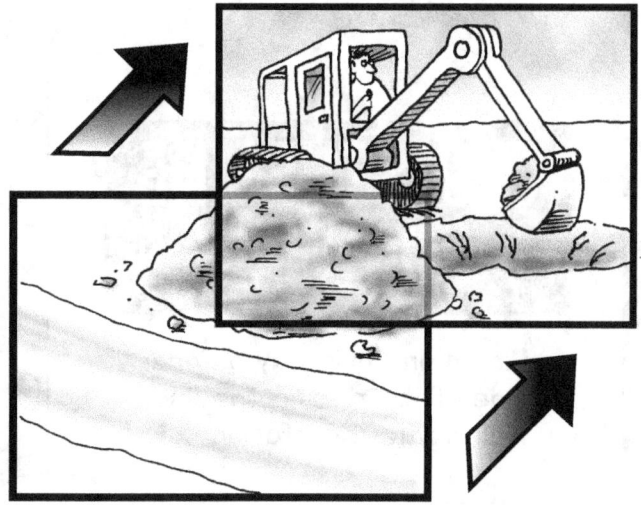

You Can Also Change focal length

Cutting to a wider or tighter shot of the same action works well for creating tension and adding visual interest. From a wide shot of the backhoe digging you can cut to a tight shot on the bucket and follow it as it dumps a load of dirt on the pile. Stay on the dirt as the bucket leaves and you then have permission to cut to another angle. It is easy to edit straight from the wide shot to the tight shot as long as the same action is included in both scenes.

What about a wipe?

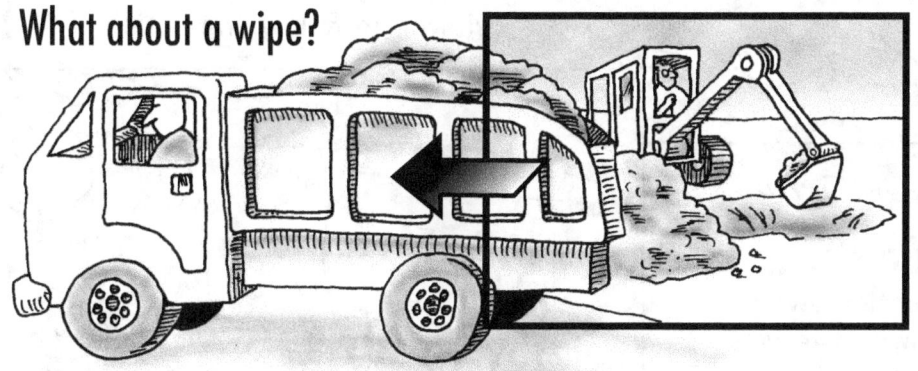

A wipe refers to something that crosses the screen revealing the action that is happening behind it. For our construction scenario we'll say we go from shooting a side angle to shooting a front angle and a dump truck drives between the camera and the backhoe. In editing, cutting as the truck is driving full frame through the scene then creates a wipe and gives the editor an interesting transition from the side angle to the front angle.

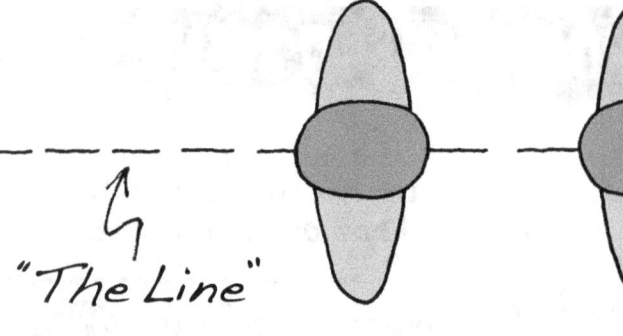

"The Line"

You can shoot from anywhere on one side, but you can't cross it.

CROSS THE LINE GO TO JAIL

Pick a line and stay on one side of it. Crossing the line will create a confusing cut.

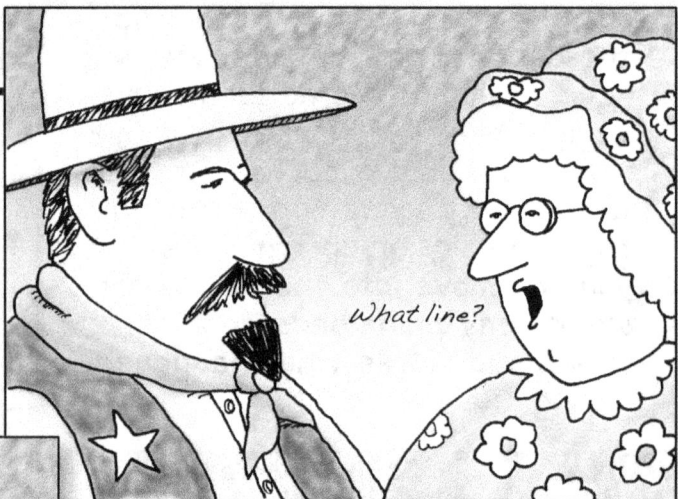

What line?

Master -- Two Shot

When shooting Over The Shoulder shots from one person to the other, making the heads the same relative size in the frame will make it much easier for the viewer to follow the action.

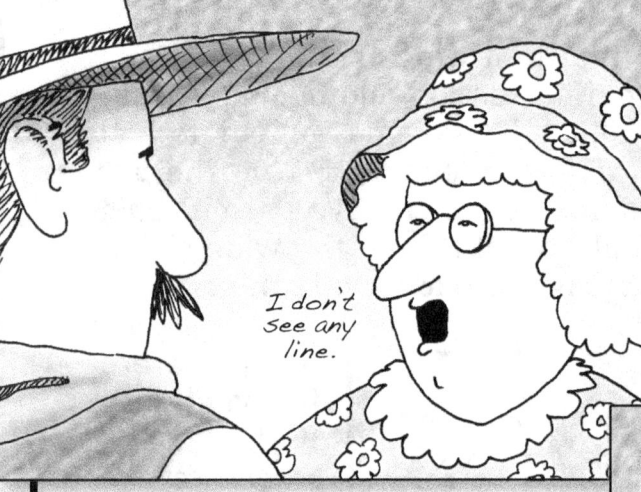

I don't see any line.

Over The Shoulder To Woman

Permission Granted...

A cutaway to action away from the scene will give you permission to change the line when you cut back to the scene.

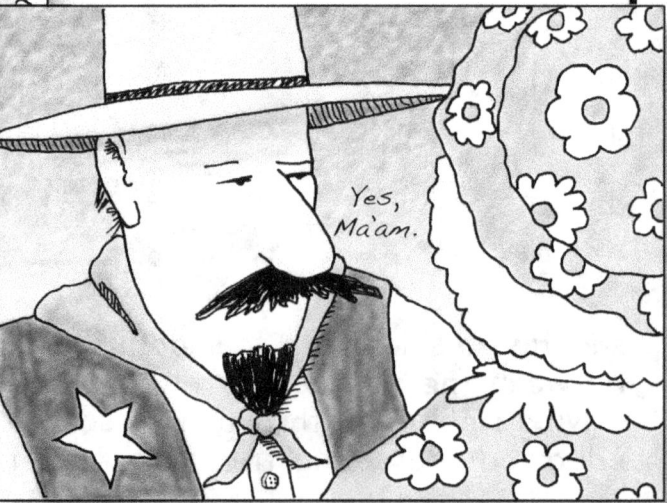

Yes, Ma'am.

POV (POINT OF VIEW)

Be aware of the role the camera plays as you shoot.
If the camera is eavesdropping on a scene it takes on the role of a casual observer. Sometimes the camera becomes the point of view of the talent—then the camera sees what the talent sees.

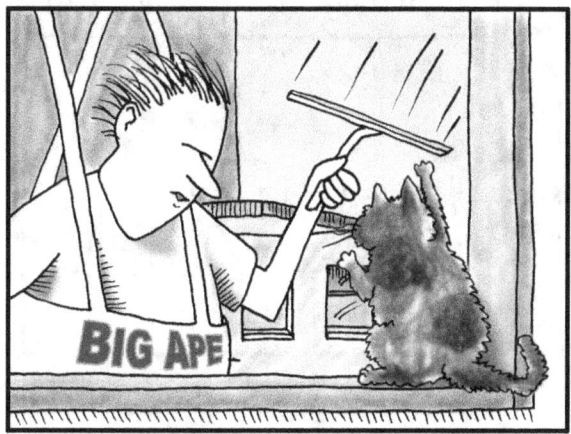

Camera as casual observer

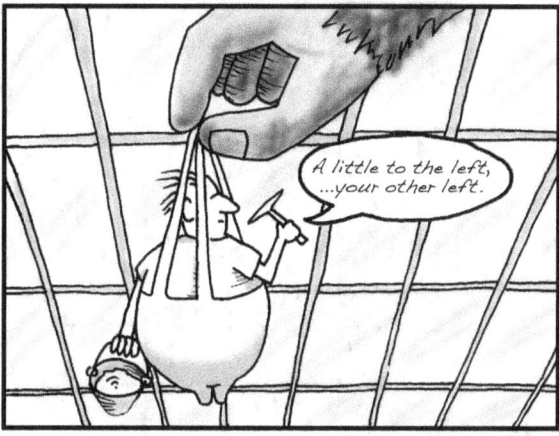

A little to the left, ...your other left.

Camera from talent POV

GASP..., some angles are more dramatic than others.

Telling the story...

In a scene with a little girl coloring at a table, you can cut to a close-up side angle of the crayon on the paper, or you can cut to her POV looking down on the drawing. Either one will work, but think in terms of which will tell the story better. If you don't want to see what she is coloring, the side angle is more dramatic. If you want to see what she is drawing, her POV will better tell the story (you can always use both).

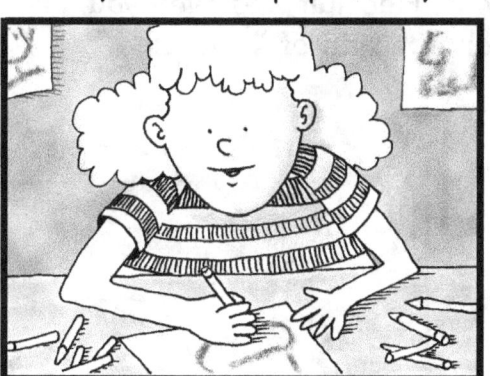

Master Shot

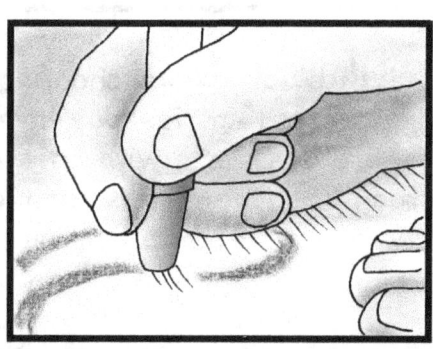

CU (Close-Up) Side Angle

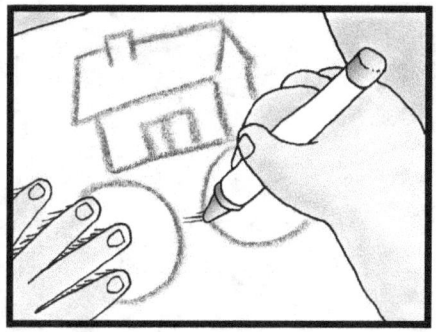

Her POV (Point Of View)

CONTINUITY

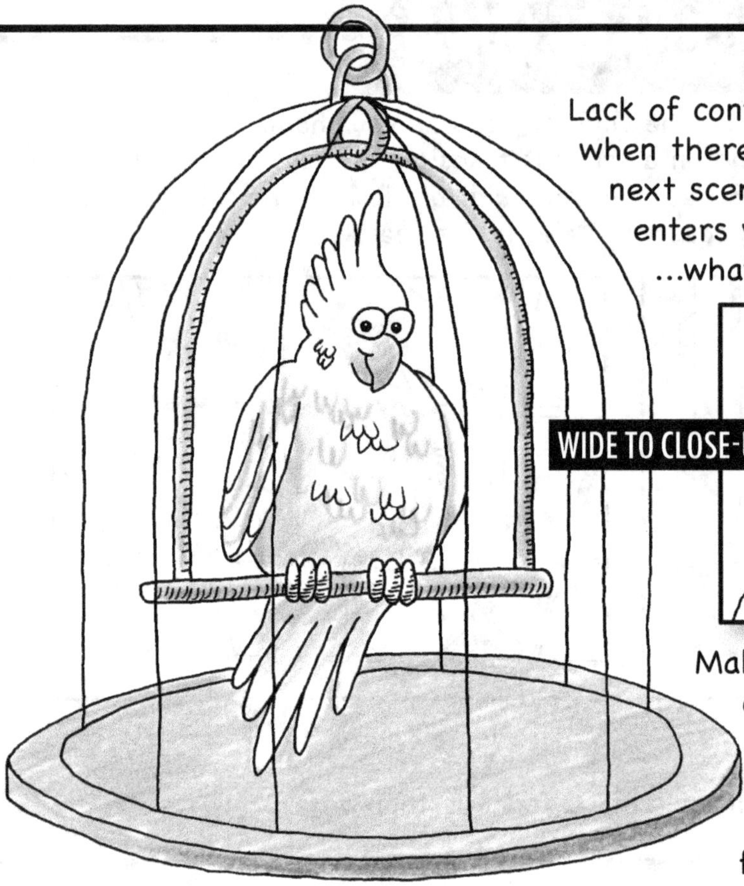

Lack of continuity becomes very obvious when there is a cut from one scene to the next scene and the first thought that enters your mind is,
...what's wrong with this picture?

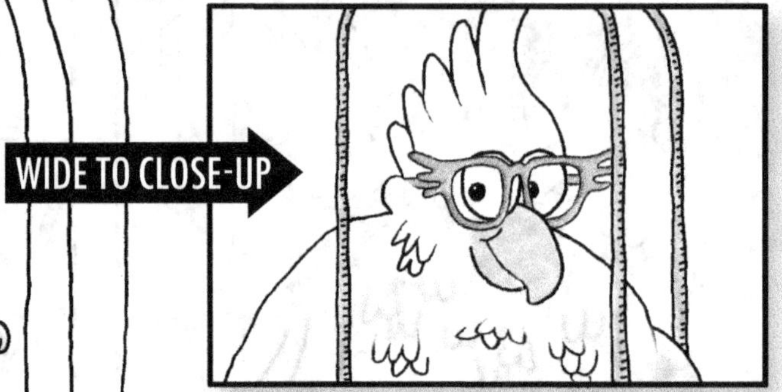

WIDE TO CLOSE-UP

Make sure to pay attention to the details from scene to scene, location to location and day to day. Cell phone cameras are a great quick reference tool for ensuring continuity.

Likewise, when shooting continuous action that involves multiple scenes with exits and entries, pay attention to how the movement is choreographed. When there is a scene with an exit from screen right, the entry to the next scene must then be made from screen left. For continuity, keep the action moving in the same direction, even if the camera angles change (low with Fido jumping over you, or running away from you) always stay on the correct side of "The Line."

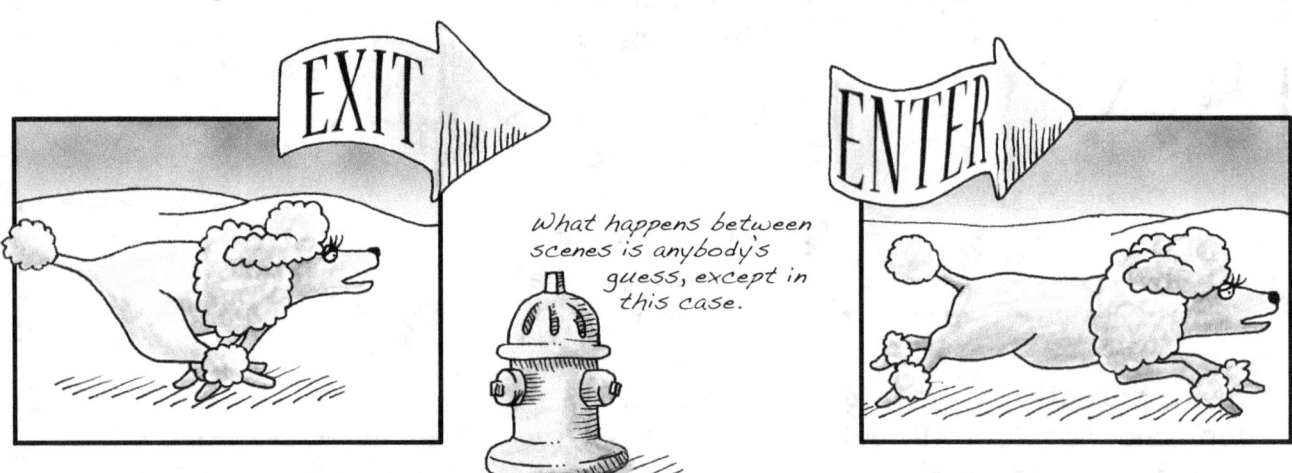

EXIT

ENTER

What happens between scenes is anybody's guess, except in this case.

CAPTURING A "MOMENT"

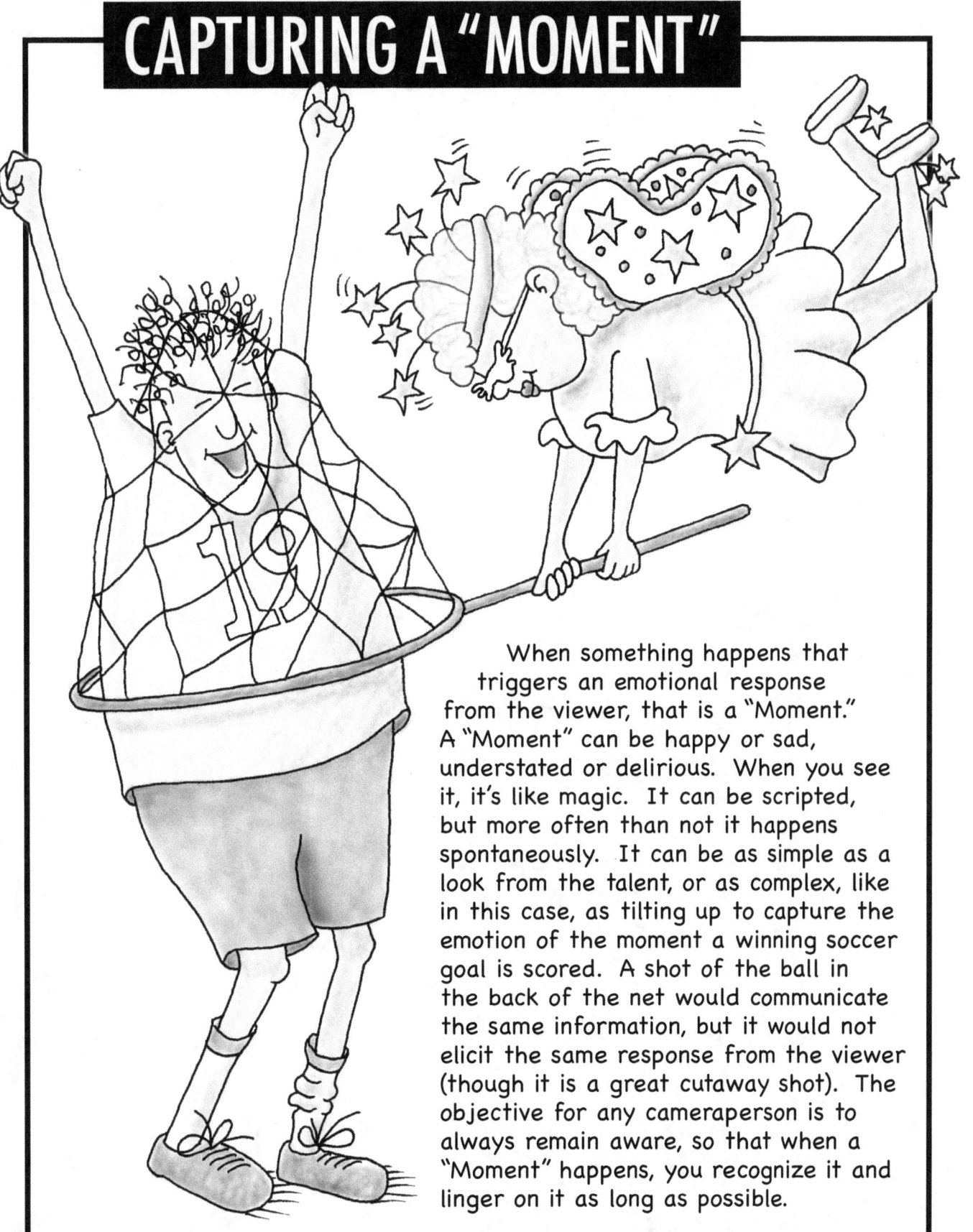

When something happens that triggers an emotional response from the viewer, that is a "Moment." A "Moment" can be happy or sad, understated or delirious. When you see it, it's like magic. It can be scripted, but more often than not it happens spontaneously. It can be as simple as a look from the talent, or as complex, like in this case, as tilting up to capture the emotion of the moment a winning soccer goal is scored. A shot of the ball in the back of the net would communicate the same information, but it would not elicit the same response from the viewer (though it is a great cutaway shot). The objective for any cameraperson is to always remain aware, so that when a "Moment" happens, you recognize it and linger on it as long as possible.

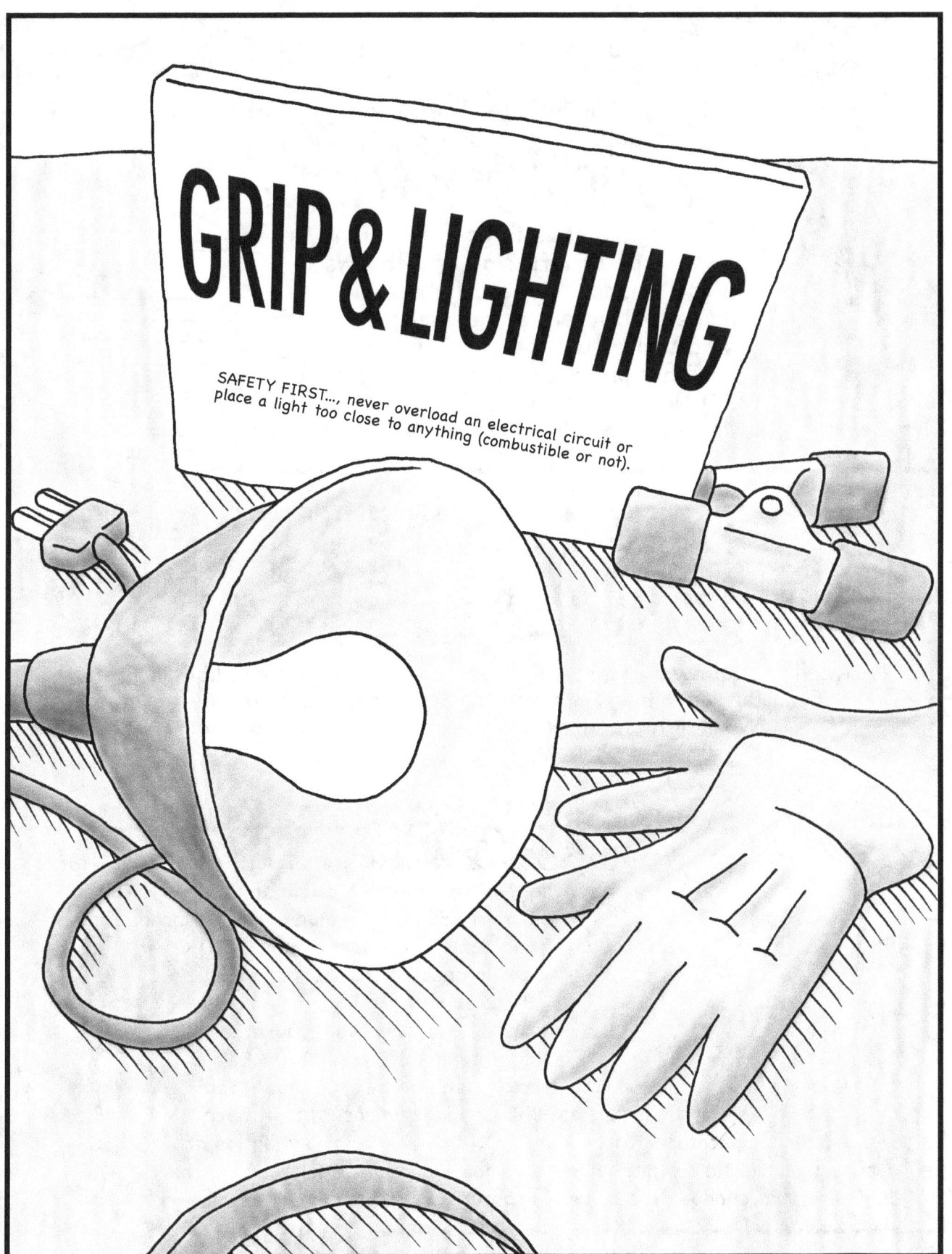

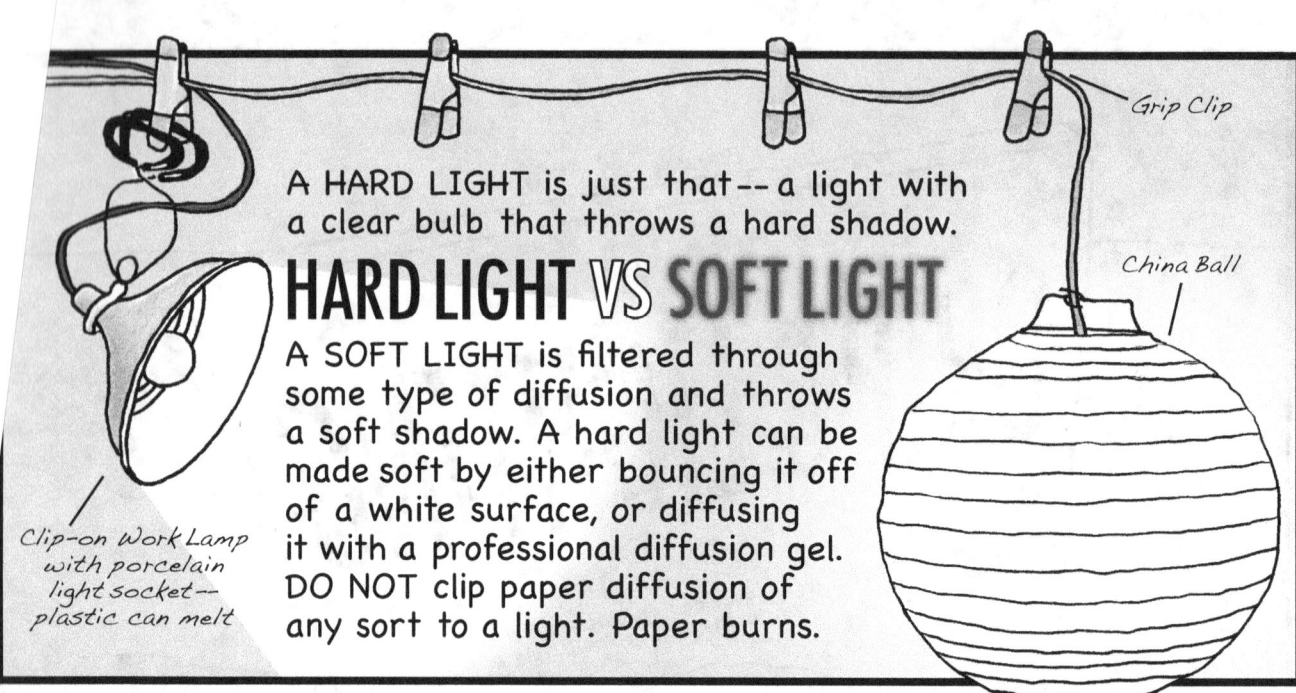

A HARD LIGHT is just that-- a light with a clear bulb that throws a hard shadow.

HARD LIGHT VS SOFT LIGHT

A SOFT LIGHT is filtered through some type of diffusion and throws a soft shadow. A hard light can be made soft by either bouncing it off of a white surface, or diffusing it with a professional diffusion gel. DO NOT clip paper diffusion of any sort to a light. Paper burns.

Grip Clip

China Ball

Clip-on Work Lamp with porcelain light socket-- plastic can melt

GRIP AND LIGHTING

Between the hardware store, photo store and Ikea you can light a feature film. But, don't buy what friends and family may already have. Work lights and extension cords (stingers) abound.

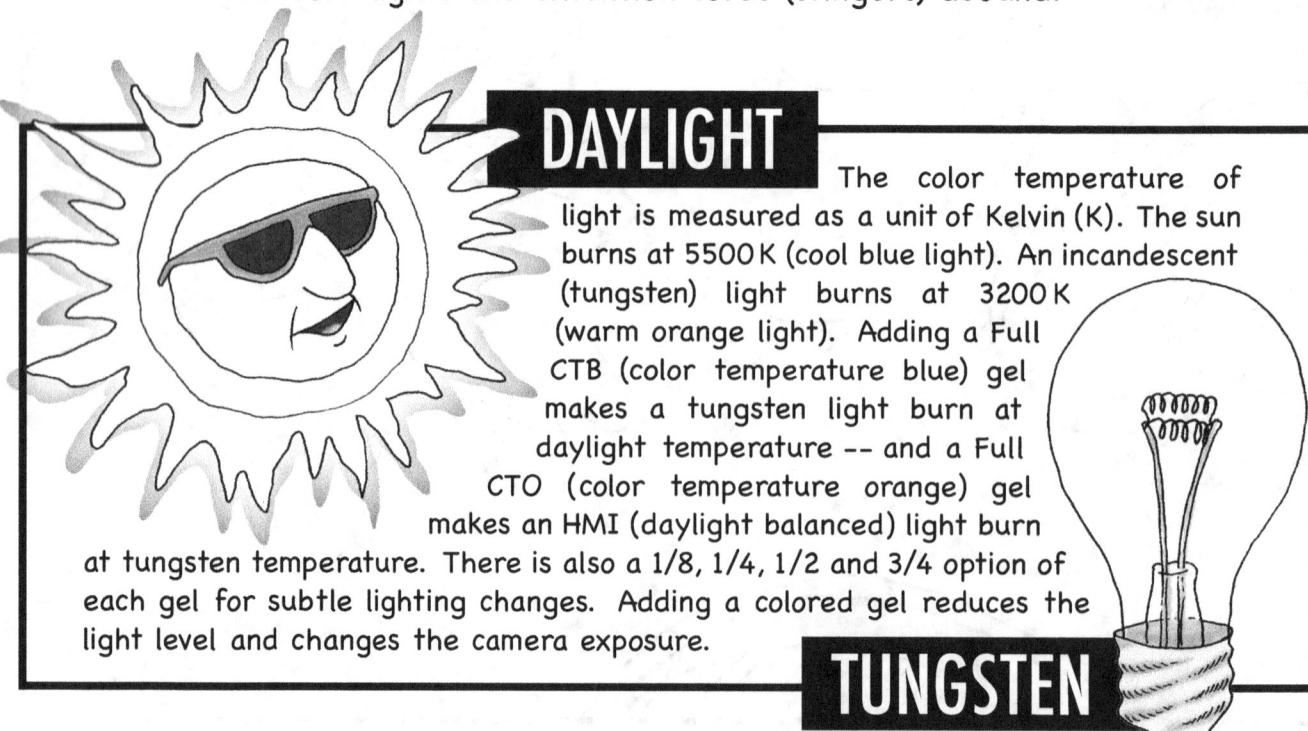

DAYLIGHT

The color temperature of light is measured as a unit of Kelvin (K). The sun burns at 5500 K (cool blue light). An incandescent (tungsten) light burns at 3200 K (warm orange light). Adding a Full CTB (color temperature blue) gel makes a tungsten light burn at daylight temperature -- and a Full CTO (color temperature orange) gel makes an HMI (daylight balanced) light burn at tungsten temperature. There is also a 1/8, 1/4, 1/2 and 3/4 option of each gel for subtle lighting changes. Adding a colored gel reduces the light level and changes the camera exposure.

TUNGSTEN

GRIP STUFF
Anything used to hold, secure, adapt or otherwise aid lighting and camera.

C-47, 47, Peg, Ammo, Bullet

The wooden clothespin is an indispensable tool for clipping a gel and/or diffusion to a light.

Grip clips hold lots of things in lots of places. And they come in an array of sizes.

GRIP CLIP

ADAPTERS

A necessity for any grip kit. They'll come in very handy.

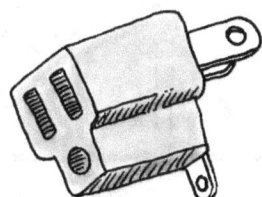

3 Prong to 2 Prong Ground Adapter

3-FER

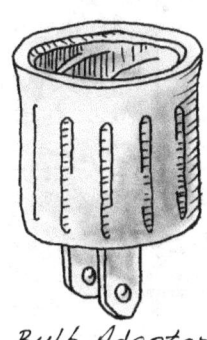

Bulb Adapter

YOU CAN NEVER HAVE TOO MANY CLIPS

CORNER TIES

Fabric is a great way to make large panels for both diffusion and reflectors. Reinforcing the corners by sewing on a backing fabric and applying grommets will help when securing the fabric with a tie down. Velcro on the corners also works, but it's not as versatile as using a rope.

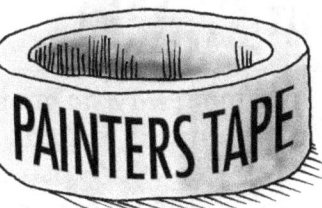

PAINTERS TAPE

A great alternative to gooey, sticky gaffers tape. Painters tape is perfect for sticking cords to the floor, or securing anything else that needs to be taped without leaving ugly tape residue.

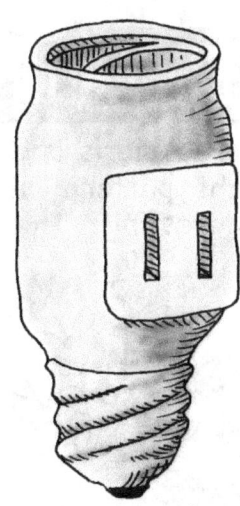

Light Socket Outlet Adapter

C-STAND

"C" for Century, because it can be used in 100 ways. (Even if it's a myth, it's the truth.) Essential to any production, it can hold cords, cables, flags, lights, blankets, reflectors, even other C-stands. The great thing is they're virtually indestructible, so they are usually easy to rent from a grip house or photo store. For safety, make sure to rent a sandbag for each stand.

GOBO Head

Arm

Knuckle

GOBO Head

On some stands the top leg is a "Rocky Mountain" leg. It slides up and down the post, enabling the stand to sit securely on an uneven surface such as a staircase.

Always use a sandbag to secure the stand.

ALERT

RIGHTY TIGHTY LEFTY LOOSEY

Make sure the tension (weight) on every gobo head knuckle is always pulling down on the tightening (right) side of the screw (clockwise). If the tension is pulling down on the loosening (left) side (counter clockwise), it will eventually unscrew, give way and fall. Also, when adjusting the arm, lower the stand to a position that is safe to work with, then raise it back up.

BREAK UP THAT WALL

A cookaloris is a very common way to mottle the light pattern on a wall to make it look more interesting. The closer the cookaloris is to the light the softer the shadows, the further away from the light the harder the shadows. Tape can also be used on the frame to simulate a window or just create a random pattern. It works best with a focused light (a fresnel or spot light). Don't place it too close to the light. It will burn.

Plastic Plant or Tree Branch

Lace Fabric

Embroidery Hoop

THE POWER OF BLACKWRAP AND ALUMINUM FOIL

SNOOT

To help direct the light, a snoot can be formed and clipped onto the front of a light. This helps when the lighting setup requires a more dramatic look.

LENSER

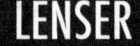

Clipping foil to the light forms a crude barn door. It blocks light from hitting the camera lens, while still allowing the light to illuminate the subject. It can also help contain or reduce spill.

FLAG/REFLECTOR

Great for blocking light from, or reflecting light into a small setup. Foil reflects a nice broken light pattern for tabletop product shots. A grip clip helps stabilize the foil.

COOKALORIS

Holes poked in the foil create a pattern as light shines on a surface (like a wall). A light that is focused works best (a fresnel or spot light).

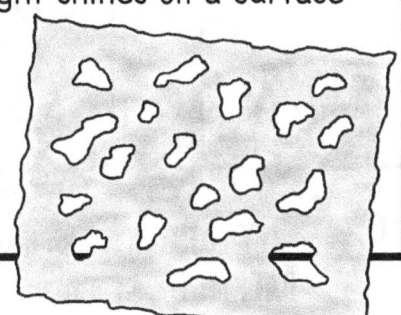

ACCENT LIGHTING

Sometimes there will be a dark hole that needs to be filled with a small light source. Just a glow behind a plant or a chair to bring out the silhouette, or a vase on a table that would look great if it had a little backlight. This rig is perfect for that. And with a dimmer, it can be easily adjusted to the correct exposure level. Big production or small, the little things can make a huge difference.

Stabilize with a Grip Clip

Bulb Adapter

Extension Cord

The first time you grab a hot light you'll understand why you need a good pair of these...

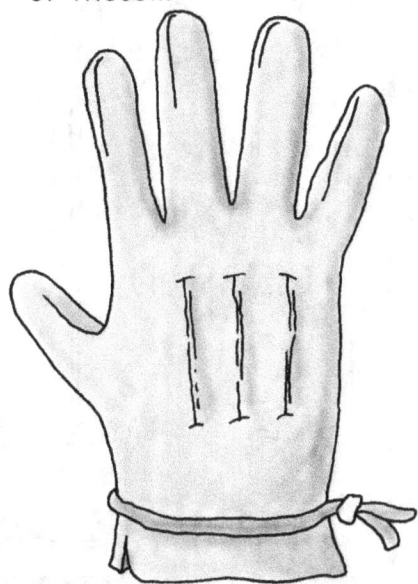

CLASSIC PORTRAIT LIGHTING

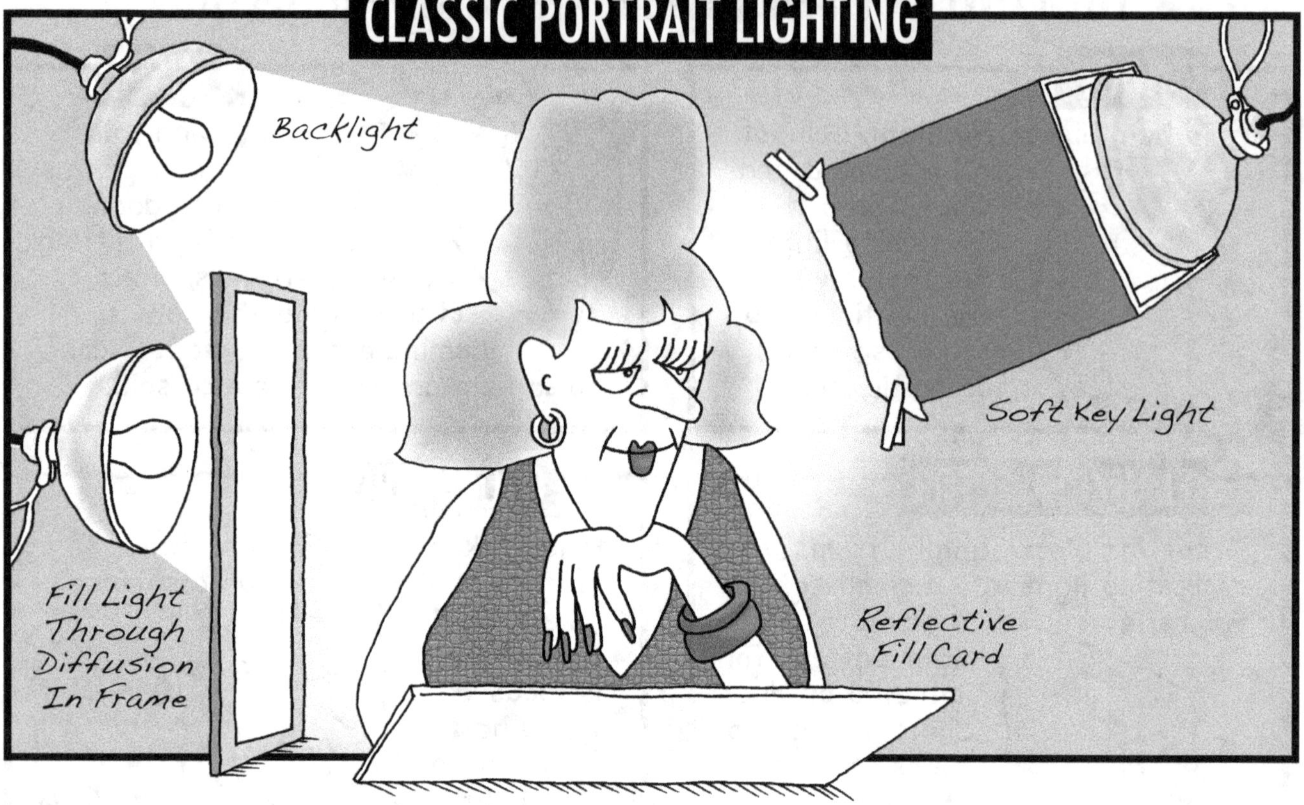

Backlight

Soft Key Light

Fill Light Through Diffusion In Frame

Reflective Fill Card

KEY LIGHT The primary light source, traditionally soft.
BACKLIGHT A rim or hair light creates definition. It can be hard or soft.
FILL LIGHT Bounce light off of a card or soften it through diffusion.

BUILD A SOFT BOX

A soft box directs the light from a wide light source into a smaller area, reducing the spill and allowing more control over where the light will fall.

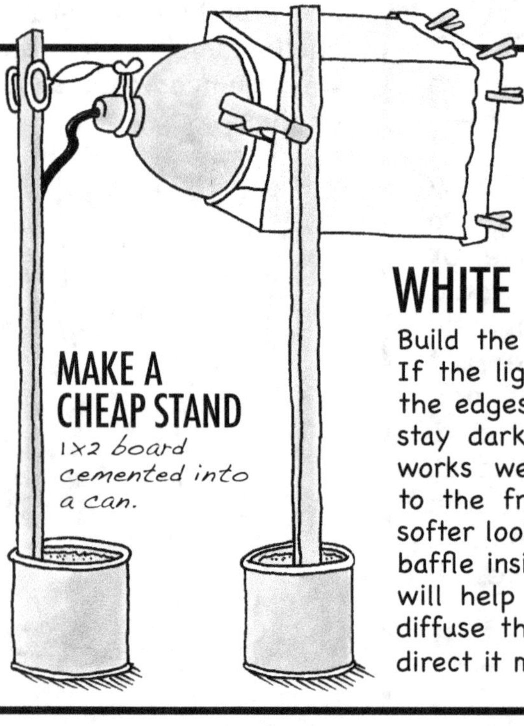

WHITE FOAMCORE AND PACKING TAPE

MAKE A CHEAP STAND
1x2 board cemented into a can.

Build the box larger than the light being used with it. If the light is larger than the box, light will spill over the edges lighting areas that should stay dark. Clip diffusion (velum works well in this application) to the front of the box for a softer look. Placing a baffle inside the box will help to further diffuse the light and direct it more to the subject.

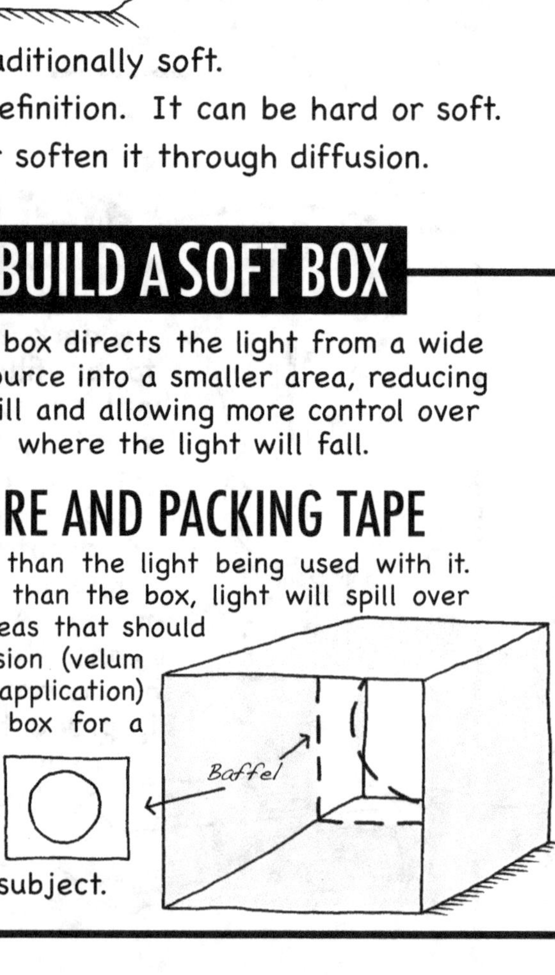

Baffel

IT WAS THE BEST OF LIGHT, IT WAS THE WORST OF LIGHT.

If you show up at noon, expect to shoot a raccoon. At that point, look for shade. Use reflectors as your key lighting elements. Overcast days can be the best because the light is so even and the shadows being cast are soft. Some fill may still be required. Learn to use the sun to your advantage. Early or late in the day is a good bet. Using the sun as a backlight is always pretty, but a bounce card may be required in front to even out the ratios.

REFLECTORS

Reflectors come in all shapes and sizes. Standard colors are white, silver and gold. Get show card at art stores, insulation panels at hardware stores, dashboard sun protectors at auto parts stores. Fabric stores have bolts of shiny material that can be sewn into larger panels. There are mirrors of all sizes (even some that won't break). Remember, the shinier the surface, the harder the shadow. For some applications, a backlight can be set and a bounce card in the front may be all that is needed for a key light.

AMBIENT LIGHT LEVELS

To subtly increase the overall light level in a room, try bouncing a light off of the ceiling or a wall.

HOLLYWOOD IT!

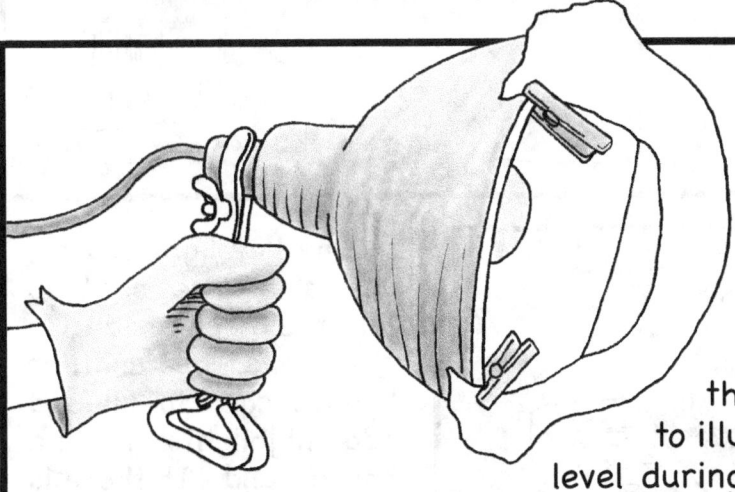

Sometimes the light needs to move with the subject. An example would be a tracking shot of the talent as they walk with the camera. Not wanting the light levels to change during the walk, the key can be carried to illuminate the subject at the same level during the entire take. Be aware of how the light plays on the surrounding environment, it should be subtle and not throw distracting shadows that will be seen as it moves. Depending on the setup, the light source can be an electrical element or a reflector.

HOW TO CONTROL LIGHT LEVELS

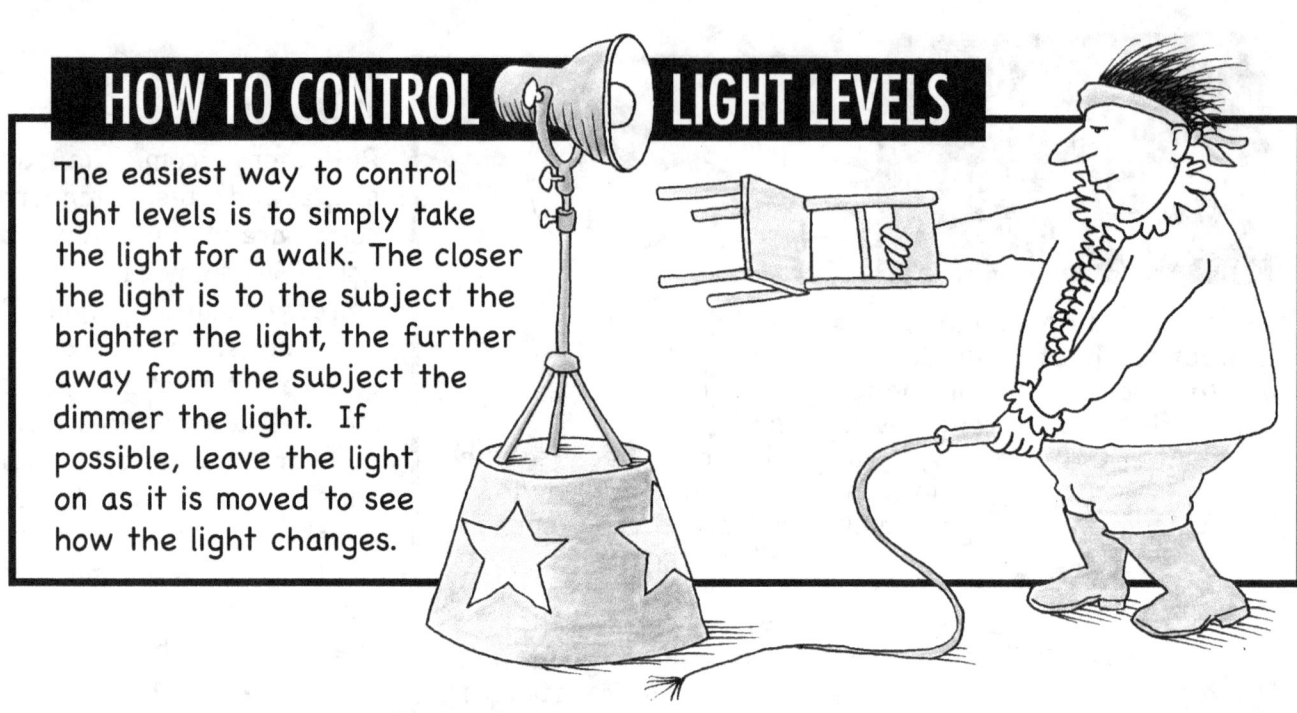

The easiest way to control light levels is to simply take the light for a walk. The closer the light is to the subject the brighter the light, the further away from the subject the dimmer the light. If possible, leave the light on as it is moved to see how the light changes.

TIME IS MONEY!
LEARN TO THINK FAST AND MOVE QUICKLY

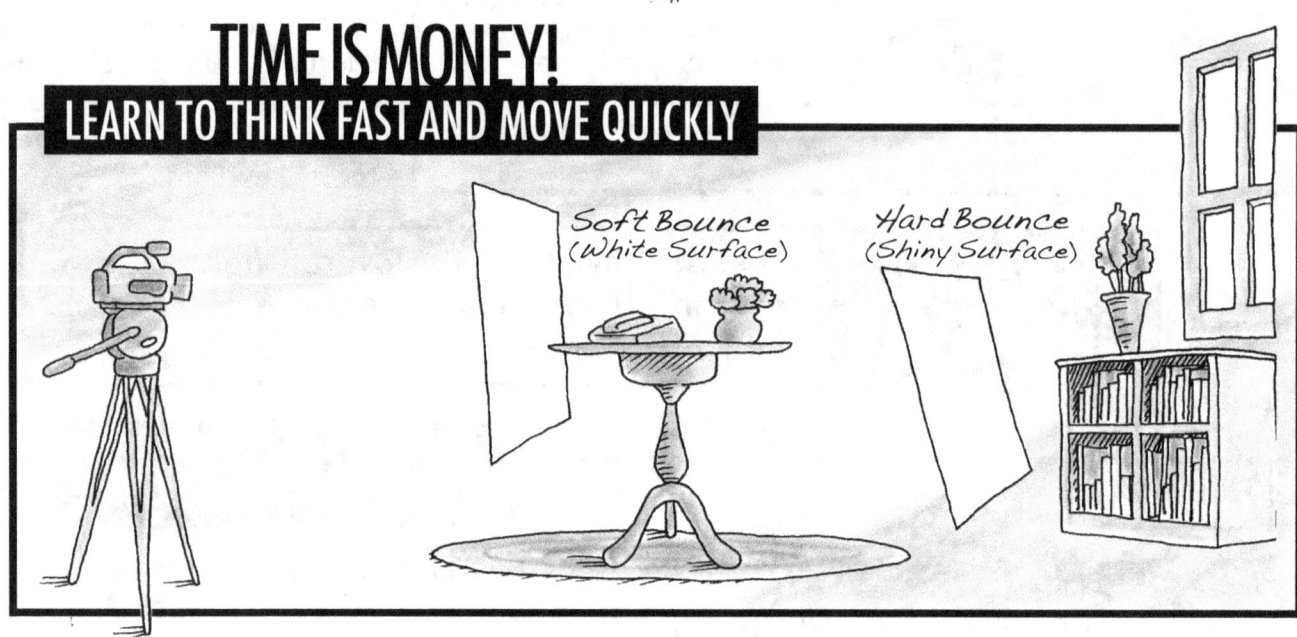

Soft Bounce
(White Surface)

Hard Bounce
(Shiny Surface)

The script calls for an insert shot of a phone being answered. Glance around the room. Sun is shining through a window and falling on a small table--perfect backlight. Set the camera as far from the table as possible, with the table as far from the background as possible. With the sun

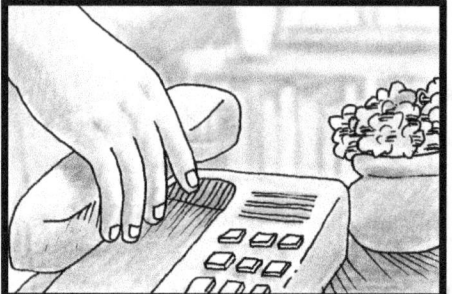

as the key light source, use a bounce card to fill the front side of the phone. Use another bounce card to fill and add highlights to the background. If there is a blind on the window, it can help control the backlight exposure level. It's a simple setup using available light and two or three reflectors.

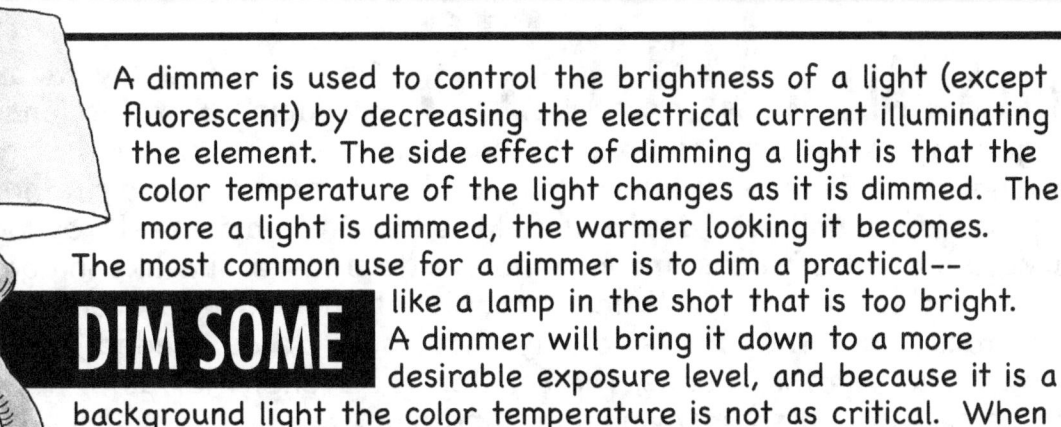

A dimmer is used to control the brightness of a light (except fluorescent) by decreasing the electrical current illuminating the element. The side effect of dimming a light is that the color temperature of the light changes as it is dimmed. The more a light is dimmed, the warmer looking it becomes. The most common use for a dimmer is to dim a practical--

DIM SOME

like a lamp in the shot that is too bright. A dimmer will bring it down to a more desirable exposure level, and because it is a background light the color temperature is not as critical. When the key light illuminating the subject is dimmed, it will start looking very orange. It is more desirable to move the key back or use a scrim (a one or two stop screen diffusion attached to the front of the light).

You're Killing Me!

Dimmers have wattage limits. If a large wattage light is put on a dimmer rated for less wattage, the dimmer will burn out.

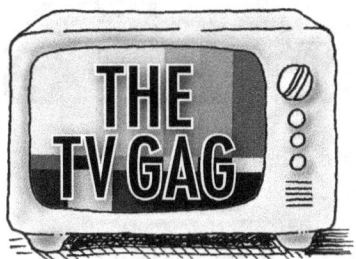

THE TV GAG

Light from a television is irregular. Images being broadcast are different in contrast and brightness. By placing a light on a dimmer in front of the television, the light can be dimmed and brightened to simulate the pattern of light that would be projected on a person watching the TV. It also works for a fireplace or campfire.

BACKLIGHT

A backlight adds dimension and creates depth. Having a rim is a great way to separate the subject from the background. To maintain detail in the highlight areas the exposure is traditionally set to no more than one and a half f-stops brighter than the key exposure, but it can be as hot (bright) as it needs to be and still look good.

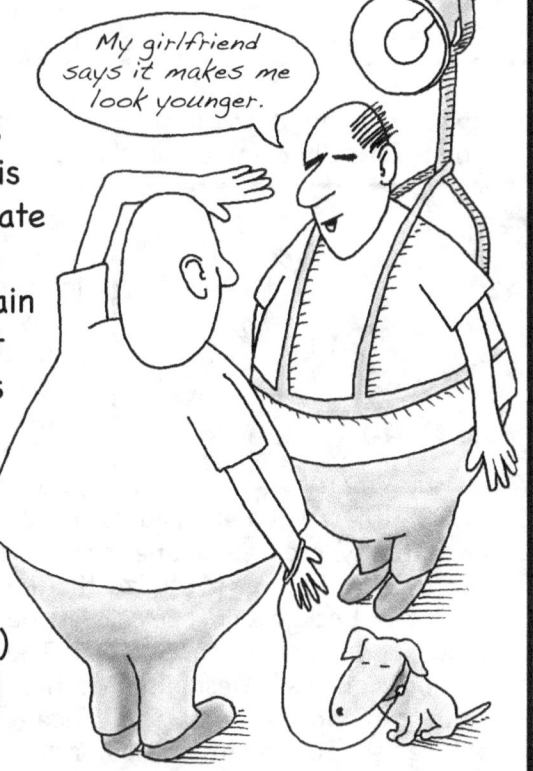

My girlfriend says it makes me look younger.

STAY SMALL to LOOK BIG

Control is the key factor to producing a professional looking image, staying as small as possible makes it easier to attain that goal. For lighting, there is less to illuminate. For the camera, by zooming in as far as possible, a shallower depth of field is easier to attain--throwing the background out of focus and helping create a more film-like image. There are always scenes that will need to be shot wide (where everything will be in focus), but the idea is to only shoot as wide as needed to make the scene work. Another bonus, the smaller the scene, the faster the scene can be set up and shot, saving time and money.

TABLETOP

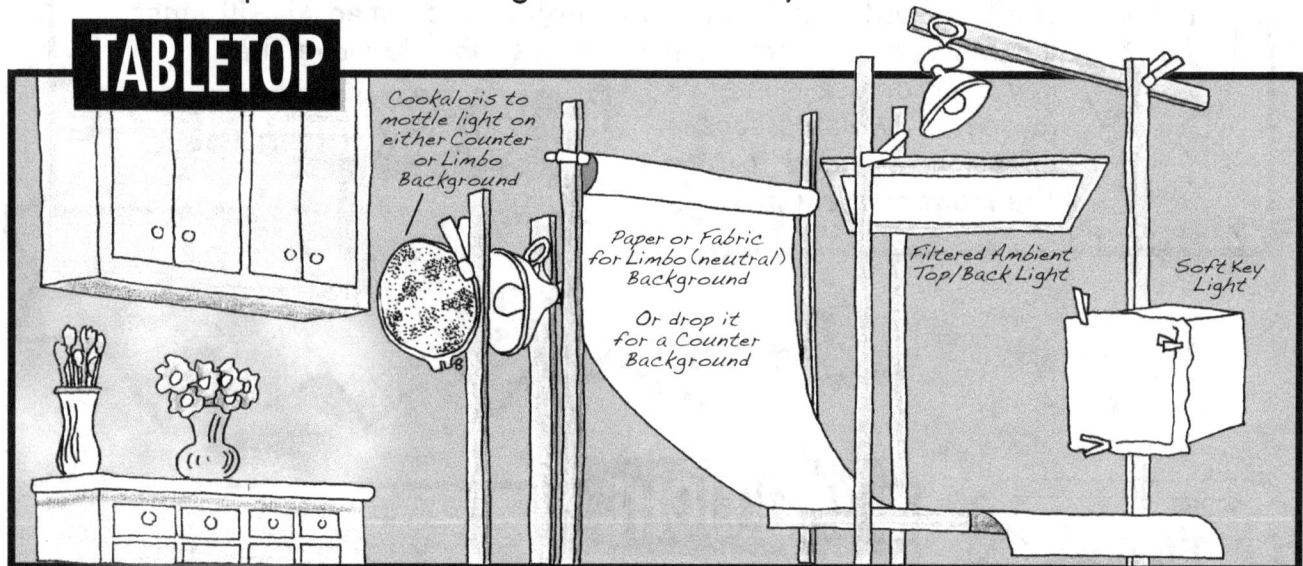

Cookaloris to mottle light on either Counter or Limbo Background

Paper or Fabric for Limbo (neutral) Background

Or drop it for a Counter Background

Filtered Ambient Top/Back Light

Soft Key Light

Tabletop is one of the most precise and time consuming styles of photography. Conceptually and stylistically a table-top shot can be on a limbo (neutral) background or in an environment.

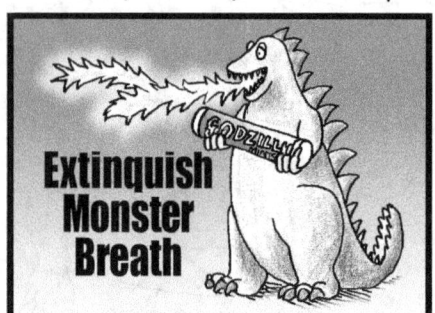

Extinguish Monster Breath

Because the product is the focus (whether it's a product package or an apple), lighting becomes critical. So, all the tricks and techniques come into play--a snoot for focusing light on a label, a cookaloris to mottle the background, bounce cards to fill areas or create a subtle or not so subtle light source. The lighting applications are usually small because the products are small. Be aware of reflections, most products have lots of shiny curved surfaces. Soft, broad light sources will help reduce hard light reflections. Think conceptually, create a shape (circle, window, abstract) to shine a hard light through to stylize the light falling on the product, or on the background. A colored gel can help separate the foreground from the background. There's a reason they call it "motion pictures." Design a shot that has action, for example,

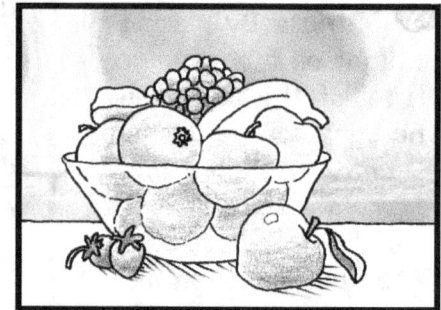

a hand setting the product in place (or pulling it out. You can reverse the footage in editing for precise placement.) Also, remember the camera-to-product-to-background distances need to be maximized with a low f-stop to create a more film-like soft focus background.

LET THERE BE LIGHT... AT DAD'S

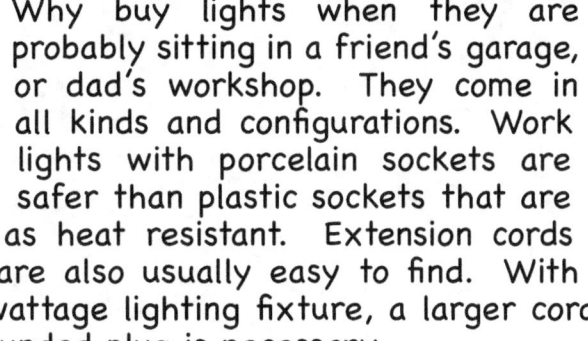

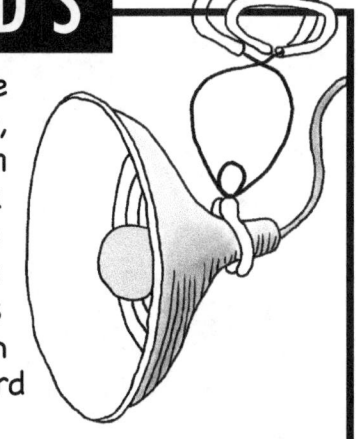

Why buy lights when they are probably sitting in a friend's garage, or dad's workshop. They come in all kinds and configurations. Work lights with porcelain sockets are safer than plastic sockets that are not as heat resistant. Extension cords (stingers) are also usually easy to find. With a higher wattage lighting fixture, a larger cord with a grounded plug is necessary.

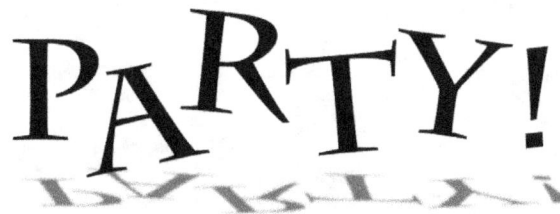

Party Gels are lighting filters that come in a variety of colors. They are intended to change the color of a light for artistic effect. Colored light can make a drab setup come to life and look much more interesting.

A wise Director of Photography once said —

"If there aren't enough lights, light the walls"

The point..., be creative and make it interesting.
Even if you have a whole truck full of lights, sometimes the absence of light or the subtle use of light delivers much greater impact to a scene.

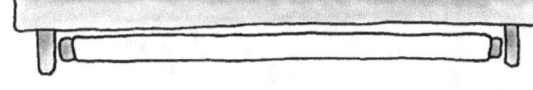

Each lighting setup will have its own set of challenges. Fluorescent lights come in cool and warm color temperatures and tend to have a greenish tint. There are gels that filter green out, or gels that will add green to tungsten or daylight. Halogen light is an entirely different color temperature. Having so many variables in a lighting setup (which most often are not that noticeable to the naked eye) is the main reason it is so important to white balance the camera for every scene. In a setup with many light sources, the different color temperatures can create an interesting look. Just make sure the white balance is taken from the Key light. Then the different colors of the background lights can become artistic texture.

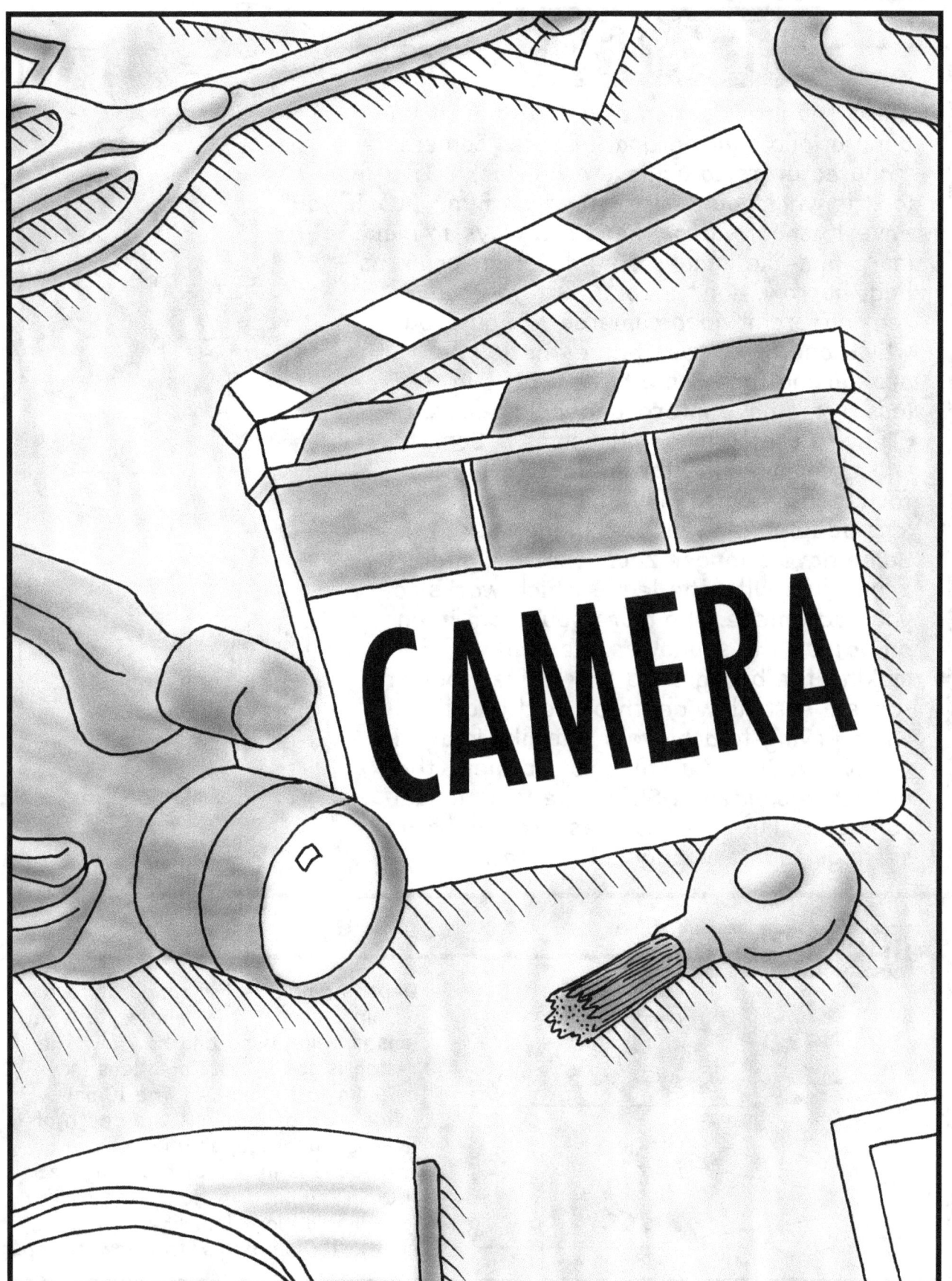

THE CAMERA

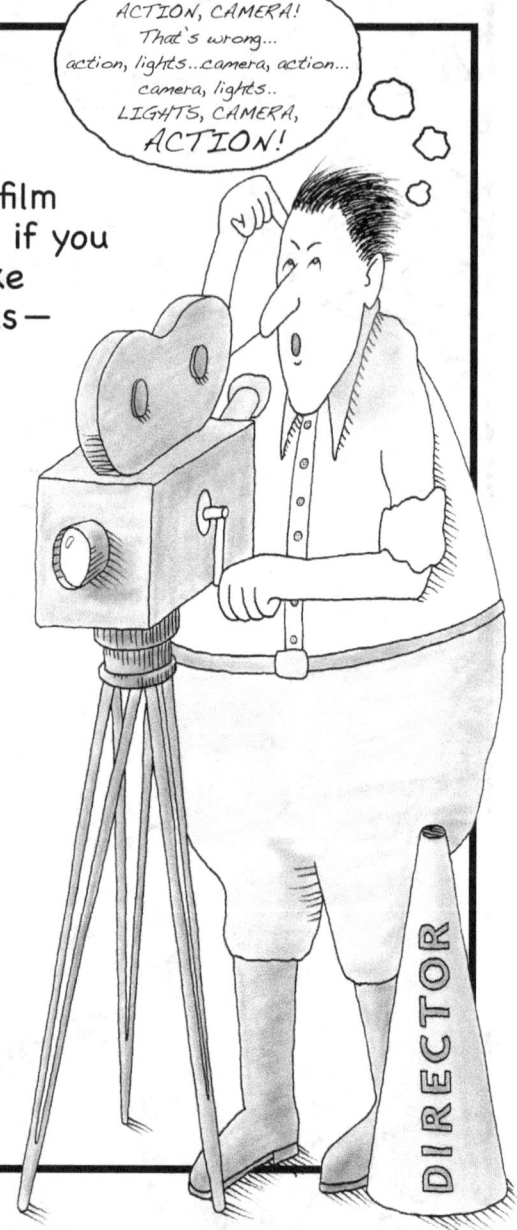

Since the introduction of video tape, it has been a long running goal of video camera manufacturers to achieve a film look. If a film look is what you desire, shoot on film. But, if you have to shoot video, there are ways to make more film-like images. Try different cameras—beg, borrow, don't steal..., but you can rent different video cameras to figure out which one gives you the aesthetic you are looking for. Some have a built-in lens; some have interchangeable lenses. (They're pretty much all zooms.) Some will accommodate a prime lens (a fixed focus lens—which may also require a lens adapter as well as a bigger budget). Some have a longer zoom (not a digital zoom, just with the lens), which works to your advantage. The more you zoom in on an object, the shallower the depth of field, making the background look softer (out of focus). A shallow depth of field is critical when trying to achieve a film-like image in video. A DSLR is a still photo camera that also shoots video. DSLRs give you manual control of film-like features, from exposure settings to interchangeable lenses.

DEPTH OF FIELD

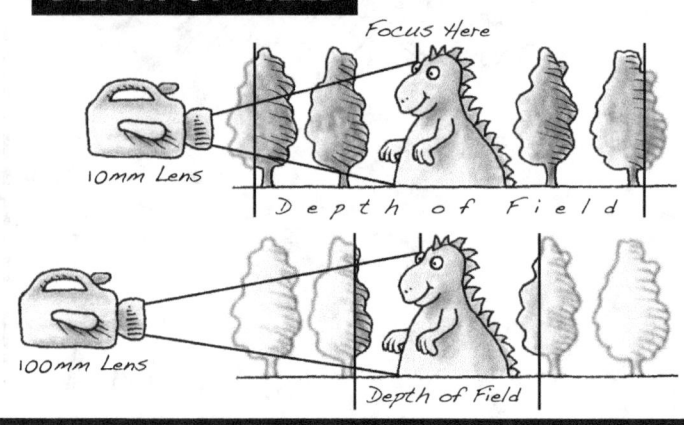

Depth of field is the range of focus within a scene; it is relative to what lens is being used and how low the f-stop is set. On a zoom lens (say a 10mm to 100mm), at the 10mm (wide) end of the lens the depth of field is much deeper (much more of the scene is in focus) than on the 100mm (zoomed in tight) end of the lens. For a more film-like image, stay on the 100mm end with a low f-stop.

27

SHOOTING FILM VS SHOOTING VIDEO

There is a difference, and knowing the basics for shooting film will give you a much better video image.

F I L M

RATIOS Ratio refers to the range of exposure from the darkest area to the brightest area of a scene.

V I D E O

Film and video see light in a different way. Film has a broader range of exposure between black and white, providing a greater variety of tonal values and creating a much more subtle image—especially in the highlight (bright) areas. Video sees more contrast in the image because it exposes from black to white much faster. This change is most evident in the brightest areas, making it critical to control the images highlight exposure. In video, exposing white and black areas more to the middle of the exposure range will give you a much better image in the end.

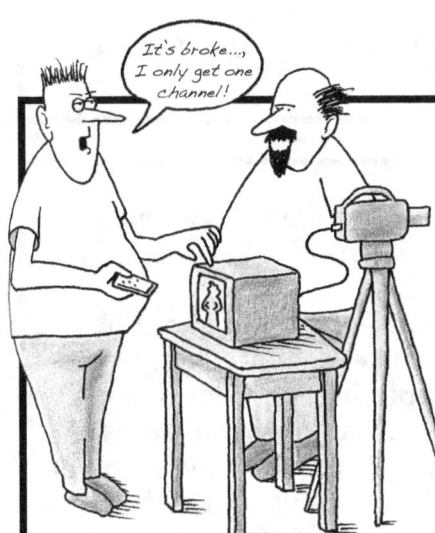

It's broke..., I only get one channel!

PROCESSING FILM AND VIDEO

The nice thing about video is that it gives you instant gratification with an image on a monitor. WYSIWYG - What You See Is What You Get. The film image, on the other hand, hides in a strip of celluloid (film negative) until it is developed. Then and only then can the D.P. (Director of Photography) see that the image actually exists and stop holding his/ her breath. Video tape is essentially ready for broadcast, but the film negative must be transferred to video tape in a telecine session. The telecine operator (colorist) color grades the film (makes it look good). The D.P. exposes the film negative within the same ratios as video tape, ensuring there is as much detail as possible in the dark and light areas of the image. This gives the colorist maximum latitude to control color and add contrast in the shadow and highlight areas.

A SIMPLIFIED FILM TO VIDEO COMPARISON

Film Speed:

FILM - Color negative film stocks are rated at a variety of speeds (ASA, aka ISO) ranging from 50 ASA to 500 ASA. The speed of the film determines how much light is needed to expose the film in a normal range. The lower the ASA/ISO number (50 ASA) the more light is required to expose the film, and conversely the higher the number (500 ASA) the lower the light requirement.

VIDEO - It is generally accepted that video is rated at 320 ASA/ISO.

Frame Rate:

FILM - Film cameras shoot sync sound (people talking) at 24 frames per second (fps). But, the camera also allows you to shoot non-sync sound at various speeds from very slow (8 fps) for a very swishy/blurry looking image, to very fast (90 fps) for slow motion. And with all things photographic, if you change the frame rate, you change the amount of light required to expose the film correctly. A quick example is if you shoot at 12 fps you will need half the light you would need for a normal 24 fps exposure, because the film is running through the camera half as fast with each frame being exposed twice as long. Conversely, if you shoot at 48 fps, you need twice as much light to expose the film running at twice the normal speed and being exposed half as long per frame.

VIDEO - Most Standard Definition (NTSC) video cameras shoot at 30 fps. Some can shoot at 60 fps and 24 fps. High Definition (ATSC) cameras can shoot at 30 fps, 60 fps and/or 24 fps.

Shutter Speed:

FILM - The shutter speed is the length of time each frame is exposed. A film camera's shutter speed is measured at 1/50 th of a second.

VIDEO - Video is optimal at 60, 1/60 th of a second -- or when shooting DSLR HD at 24p, 50, 1/50th of a second. But, unlike a film camera, the shutter speed on a video camera is variable, which allows some creativity in shooting. If the camera is set to a slower shutter speed (1/15 th) the image has the same look as shooting a lower frame rate on film—any motion has a swishy/blurry quality. On the other end of the spectrum (1/1000 th), the image becomes very sharp and makes normal action appear to stutter. Faster shutter speeds are designed to shoot high speed activities like car racing. Slow motion is controlled in editing. And remember, any shutter speed change will require an exposure change to adjust the need for more or less light.

READING LIGHT

Whether you are shooting film or shooting video, think ratios. Knowing how the camera sees the light is critical to a first class image.

Film and video cameras use f-stops to see light. Like the iris of an eye, the more open the aperture of the lens, the more light is exposing the image. Typical f-stop settings for a lens can range from a wide open setting (for low light) at f 2.0 to a closed down setting (for bright light) at f 22. RATIO refers to the exposure range between the hottest (brightest) area and the darkest area of a scene. It is critical to control the ratios to ensure the detail of the image is maintained. In a nutshell, at whatever f-stop the subject is exposed, the brightest area should be no more than one and a half stops brighter. And the dark areas should not be exposed more than one and a half stops darker.

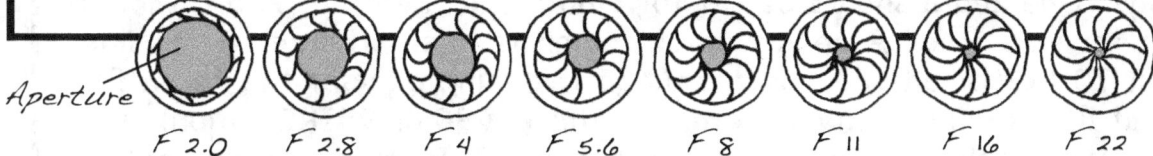

Aperture

F 2.0   F 2.8   F 4   F 5.6   F 8   F 11   F 16   F 22

HOW TO USE A LIGHT METER

Incident Light Meter

An incident light meter reads the light falling on a scene. There are settings you will need to know to compute a light meter reading. Though used primarily for film and DSLRs, for a video camera the meter would be set to:

ASA/ISO: 320
ShutterSpeed: 1/60
(for a frame rate of 30/60fps)

To take a reading, place the meter just in front of the subject and point it at the camera. It will tell you what the camera's f-stop should be set to for the key light. To measure the backlight level, from the subject point the meter in the direction of the light you want to measure. For the correct ratio it should read no more than one and a half stops brighter than the key light (i.e.- key at f 4.0, backlight at f 5.6 5).

FOR VIDEO, ZEBRAS ARE YOUR BEST FRIEND

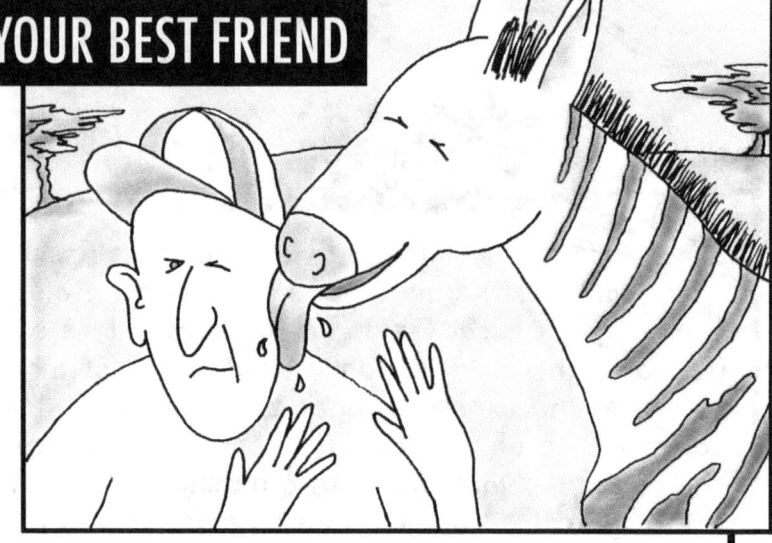

The zebra settings in a video camera function the same way a light meter functions when shooting film. Zebras provide a range of technical information to determine the exposure of the image. Video cameras measure light in I.R.E. Units (named for the Institute of Radio Engineers), with 100 IRE being white and 0 IRE being black. Cameras typically provide an option for two zebra settings. One zebra should be set for white, and the other zebra should be set for skin tone. A good rule of thumb is to set the zebra for skin tone at 70 IRE (small pools of zebras on the skin), and set the zebra for white at 100 IRE (high-end cameras may have a 90 or 95 IRE option). For cameras with only one zebra setting, use 100 IRE for maximum control of the highlights. Video cameras don't like really bright images. The loss of detail in the highlight areas tends to make them bloom and look very odd. When lighting, once the exposure for white and skin tone have been set, light the rest of the scene so it looks good to the eye and on the monitor. (A really good monitor makes all the difference.) Make sure to keep the exposure ratios within the critical levels. The goal is to expose the overall image more toward the middle of the exposure range. (That does not mean light it flat. Build in contrast, but try to not make it too extreme.) Just as the colorist grades the film in telecine, the correct exposure will give you the freedom in post production (editing) to control the black and white detail levels.

70 IRE

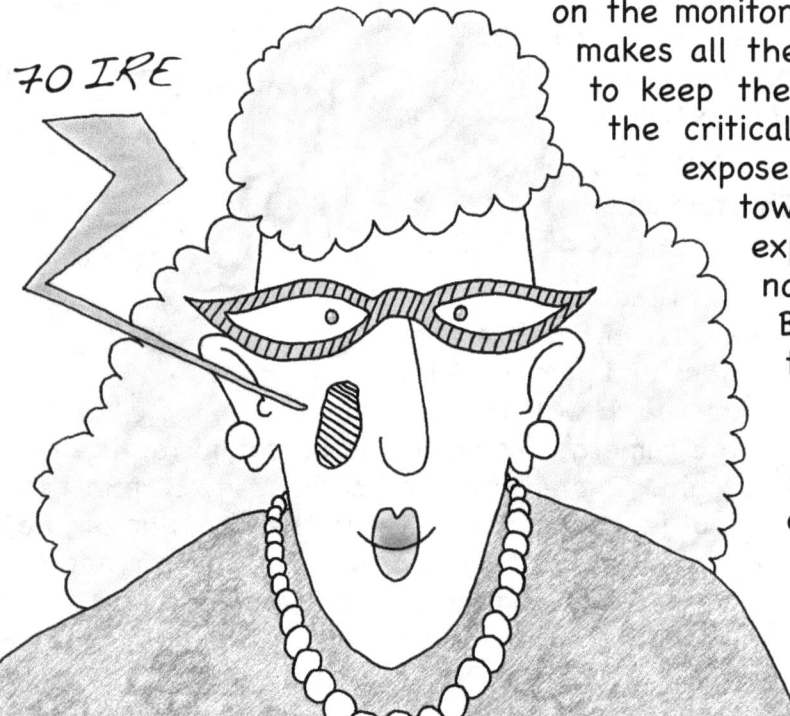

WHITE BALANCE

A video camera uses white to balance the color of the light falling on a subject. Cameras have built-in white balance settings (daylight and tungsten). But sometimes there are multiple sources lighting the subject; a little daylight (blue), a little tungsten (orange). So you need a custom white balance to ensure the correct color balance where white is actually white. To white balance, zoom in on a white sheet of paper so it fills the frame in the same position as the subject (exposed at just under 100 IRE). This will ensure the white card is reflecting all of the light sources falling on the subject, then set the white balance. If you are using a filter on the lens, white balance before you apply the filter.

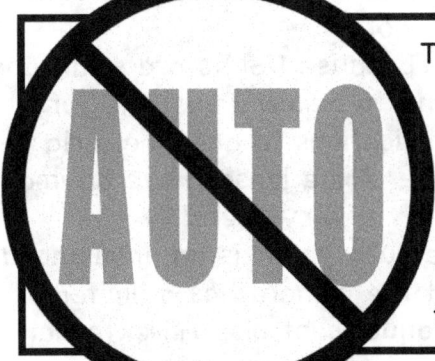

The camera should never be set to auto. Learn to manually control the camera functions.

When shooting outside, the sun can be an overwhelming light source. Most video cameras have built-in ND (Neutral Density) filters that help control the exposure by essentially putting sunglasses on the lens. There are usually two settings, one lighter and one darker. A film camera will need a filter applied in front of the lens. Film filters come in ND3 (one stop), ND6 (two stops), and ND9 (three stops). A neutral density filter not only helps control light levels, but also allows the camera to shoot at a lower f-stop. The lower the f-stop, the shallower the depth of field, helping create that ever desirable film-like look.

NEUTRAL DENSITY FILTERS

When shooting inside during the day, windows present a considerable challenge. Without a very strong HMI light source (daylight balanced), it is difficult to keep the inside exposure close to the outside exposure, making anything seen through a window a bright indistinguishable glow. The obvious solution is to not have a window in the shot. Another is to apply a ND (Neutral Density) gel to the window to bring the outside exposure down closer to the interior exposure. ND gels come in the same 3, 6, and 9 densities as camera filters, and can be trimmed to fit the widow shape.

DSLR

Digital Single-Lens Reflex

A DSLR is a still photo camera that also shoots video. There are many DSLRs to choose from that shoot video in a variety of formats from Standard Definition (480i) to High Definition (1080p). Single-lens reflex refers to a series of mirrors that reflect the image the lens sees to the viewfinder, in the back, so your eye can see it. When you push the button to take a still photo the mirror flies up out of the way and exposes the image on a digital sensor behind it. Video uses live preview, where the mirror is always out of the way and the image is viewed on an LCD monitor on the back of the camera.

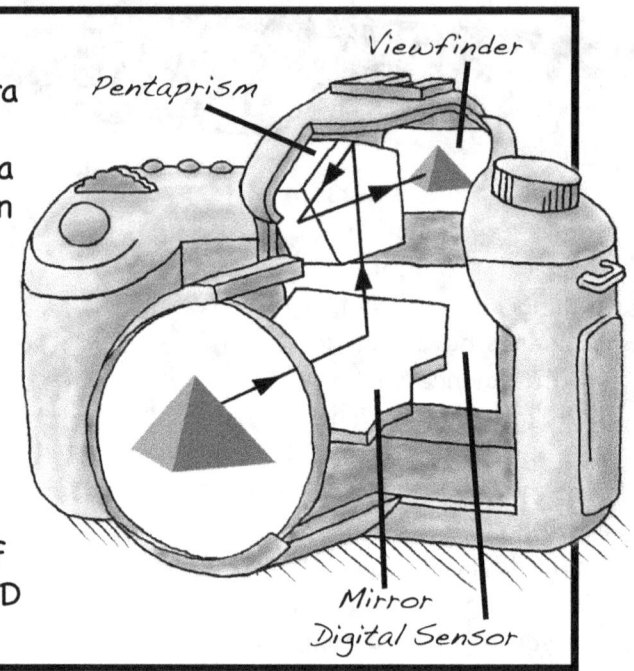

Pentaprism
Viewfinder
Mirror
Digital Sensor

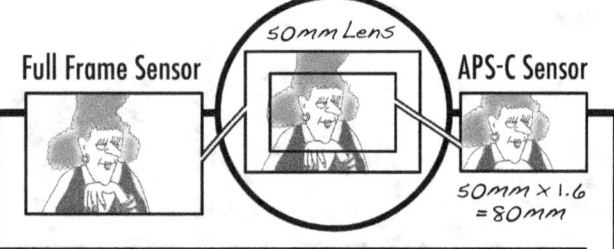

Full Frame Sensor
50mm Lens
APS-C Sensor

50mm x 1.6
= 80mm

HEY, YOUR PICTURE IS BIGGER...

The camera's digital sensor gathers the optical information seen through the lens and translates it into an electronic signal, thus creating the digital image. Sensors for high-end cameras differ slightly but commonly use one of two sizes, a full frame sensor (approximately the same size as 35mm film), and a slightly smaller sensor (APS-C). Both provide excellent image quality. But, using the same lens, the APS-C sensor "sees" less (crops the image). This "Crop Factor" differs slightly with each camera manufacturer. For this example, we'll use 1.6. So, on a camera with an APS-C sensor, a 50mm lens (multiplied by 1.6) is equivalent to using an 80mm lens on a camera with a full frame sensor.

PROS DSLRs are small, light, and record high quality images. They allow manual exposure control and have interchangeable lenses, making it much easier to control the depth of field — giving you that much-coveted film-like image.

CONS **NO ARTICULATING VIEWFINDER** ...The LCD monitor on the back is small and not easily accessible for viewing while shooting, making "Run and Gun" style production very difficult.

FOCUS... The optical focus assist function is only accessible when the camera is not recording, and since depth of field is often very shallow, it can be difficult to maintain focus when shooting.

STABILITY... Because DSLRs are small and light they tend to be very unstable for hand-held applications (a hand-held rig is a great asset). Some lenses have an image stabilizer which is very useful.

AUDIO... The audio input is an unbalanced mini plug and the camera has a limited number of manual controls. An external audio recorder is recommended.

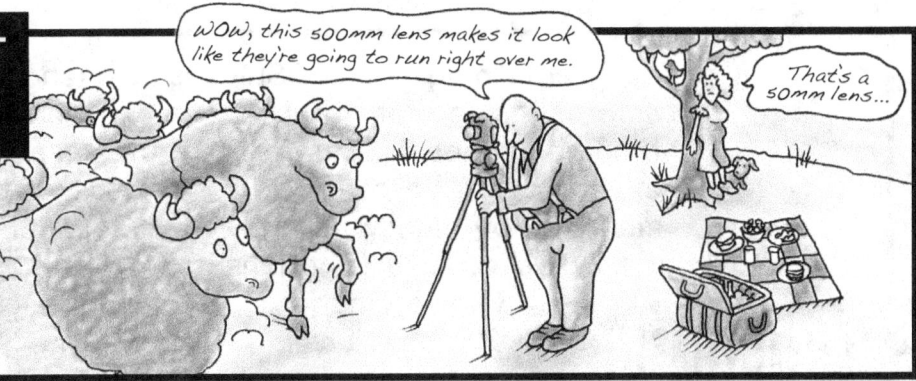

SHHHH... THE SECRET IS IN THE LENSES

DSLR cameras use interchangeable prime and zoom lenses (the same type lens a motion picture camera uses). Primes come in fixed focal lengths (35mm, 50mm, etc.) — the smaller the number, the wider the image. A zoom lens gives you the ability to change the focal length without having to physically change the lens. Zooms on DSLRs do not work the same way a zoom on a video camera works. On a video camera zooming in and grabbing focus then zooming back out will give you sharp focus throughout the entire zoom range. There is no zoom control button on a DSLR, the zoom is controlled by a ring on the lens. When you change the focal length (say you zoom from 100mm to 50mm) the focus will change, as well. Most cameras have a focus assist that enables you to optically zoom in for focusing purposes only, but you are not able to use it during recording — you must stop shooting for it to function. Auto focus is very slow and not recommended. It is always faster and more reliable to focus manually. A primary distinction for each lens is the speed of the lens. A fast lens will

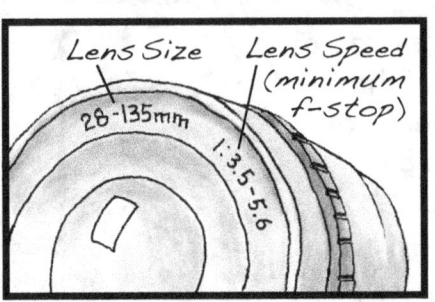

Lens Size — 28-135mm

Lens Speed (minimum f-stop) — 1:3.5-5.6

shoot in low light (f 1.4), whereas a slower lens will require more light (f 3.5). Faster lenses are commonly more expensive than slower lenses. The minimum f-stop on most zoom lenses will also change with the focal length. As illustrated, full wide (28mm) will be faster (f 3.5) than the longer end of the lens (135mm) which will be slower (f 5.6).

EXPOSURES

Using a Light Meter is the most reliable way to judge the exposure of an image. (See page 30.) High-end DSLR cameras usually have a histogram option.

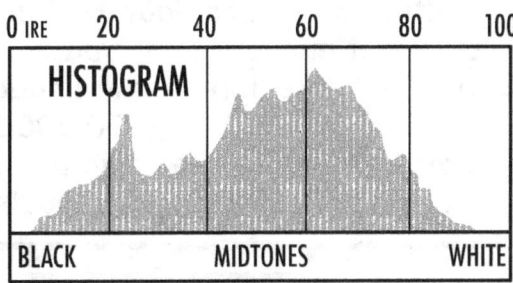

| 0 IRE | 20 | 40 | 60 | 80 | 100 |

HISTOGRAM

BLACK   MIDTONES   WHITE

Setting the histogram to brightness (not RGB) will help reinforce your light meter reading and also provide a good way to evaluate the overall exposure when you do not have a light meter. The diagram above illustrates an even exposure. Too much to the left (black) side of the graph indicates a dark, grainy image. The more to the right (white) side, the more overexposed the image. Thinking of the graph in terms of IRE units (see page 31), is a great way to insure the white areas of your image do not exceed 100 IRE. Keeping the white levels closer to 90 IRE will help ensure you maintain detail in the brightest areas.

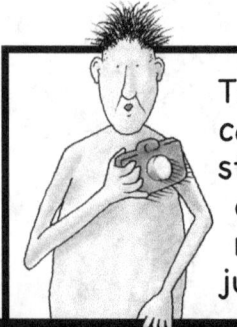

CONTROLLING YOUR EXPOSURE

The great thing about DSLR cameras, aside from their stunning images, is that the exposure can be controlled manually by manipulating just a few camera functions. (Review page 29 for a basic understanding of each component.)

ISO: The ISO is the speed of the film. Shooting at the lowest ISO possible (50, 100,...) will help minimize the grain/digital noise (multicolored speckles) in the image. If you find yourself in a situation where your f-stop will not give you enough light, you can increase the ISO to brighten the image. But, the higher the ISO (800, 1000,...) the more noticeable the grain pattern.

SHUTTER SPEED: The shutter speed is the length of time each frame is exposed as it is recorded. The shutter speed for a DSLR is ideal at 60 (1/60th of a second) or 50 for 24p. Changing the shutter speed is another way to compensate for too much or too little light (lower numbers, 30, expose each frame longer, making the image brighter -- higher numbers, 1000, expose each frame shorter, making the image darker) Just be aware of how changing the shutter speed will also affect the picture quality.

F-STOP: The f-stop helps control the depth of field. The lower the f-stop (f 2.8) the shallower the depth of field (background softer- more out of focus). When shooting outside in bright light, use an ND filter or a polarizing filter to help lower the f-stop and reduce the depth of field.

TIME-LAPSE

Intervalometer

00:00:00

Because a DSLR is first and foremost a high quality still camera, it is ideal for shooting timed exposures. Time-lapse is a series of still photos showing something that happens slowly in real time (a flower growing, or clouds moving across the sky) appear to magically happen much faster. Time-lapse photography may require an intervalometer, a device that tells the camera to take a picture at a specific interval over a set period of time. Some of the basic functions an intervalometer can control are how often a photo will be taken, how long each exposure will be (exposures at night need to be much longer), and the duration of the entire sequence. The resulting series of still photos can then be made into a movie by importing them into the editing program as an image sequence. It takes a fair amount of experimenting to adjust the intervalometer settings and camera settings so the final movie looks smooth and correctly exposed.

A FUNDAMENTAL VIDEO CHECK LIST

Every time you move the camera to a new setup
there is a series of things to double check.

CHECK THE LENS — There is nothing more amateurish than having light hit the lens and seeing how filthy it is. If you don't know the proper way to clean a lens, go to a camera store — they'll teach you.

CHECK THE LIGHT FILTER SETTING — There are, at a minimum, two settings, daylight and tungsten. Make sure the camera is set to the correct one.

CHECK THE GAIN — The gain should be set to 0. Gain (+3, +9) electronically adds light to a dark image to achieve a brighter light level. Adding gain also adds video noise in the form of a rainbow colored grain pattern. Bad.

CHECK THE WHITE BALANCE — You can run into a lot of weird lighting setups (even in one room). So, always white balance each scene (unless you are using the same lights and you are sure there is no extraneous light source bleeding into the scene). A white sheet of paper or 18% grey card works well. A color chip chart also provides a consistent white balance. After white balancing, record a few seconds of the color chart to use in editing to help balance the color from scene to scene.

CHECK THE EXPOSURE — Use the camera's zebra settings to make sure the exposure levels for the entire scene are within the ratios.

CHECK THE FOCUS — Especially if you are moving fast, this point is critical. Sometimes everything looks sharp in the viewfinder, but the viewfinder image is so small it is hard to tell. Double and triple check it.

Make sure the eyepiece viewfinder (ground glass in film cameras) is focused to YOUR eye. If the technical data you see on the viewfinder screen is out of focus and you focus the lens, the recorded image will be out of focus. Be aware of anyone stepping in to look at the scene and focusing the viewfinder to their eye — check it every time you look in the eyepiece.

CAMERA SUPPORT

A common notion with small digital video cameras is that a little tripod with a small fluid head is all you need. Wrong. The bigger the head, the better. Because the cameras are so light, it takes a larger, heavier fluid head to ensure smooth moves when panning and tilting. Unless the project calls for a more organic hand-held style, the camera should act as an anonymous observer. If the camera is jerky or hits a bump in the middle of a move, it looks like a mistake, calling attention to itself and away from the screen action.

☆ To make editing easier, record for ten seconds before starting a camera move, and settle for ten seconds at the end of the move before cutting.

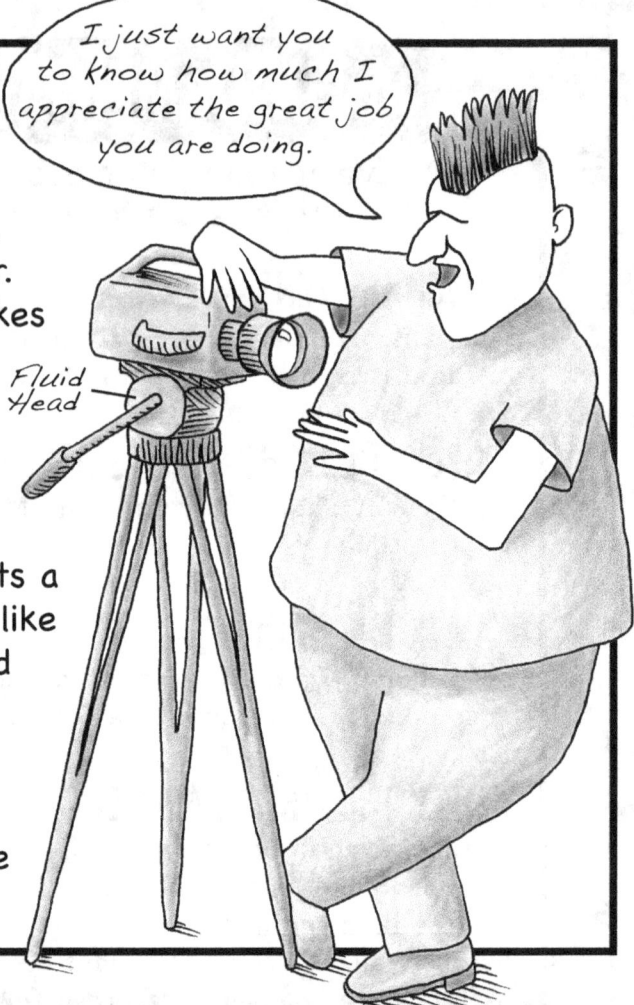

I just want you to know how much I appreciate the great job you are doing.

Fluid Head

HOW TO BUILD A HAND-HELD RIG

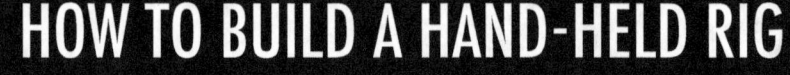

Hand-holding a small video camera is difficult, even with the stabilizer turned on, because there is no way to support the camera to keep it steady. By building a simple rig, the camera can be securely mounted to a board with a standard 1/4"-20 screw. With one end placed on the shoulder and other end held by a dowel, a stable system is created-- leaving the right hand free to operate the necessary camera controls.

1 x 4 Board

Dowel

IN THE INTEREST OF ANGLES

Don't limit the camera angles to just what can be shot from the sticks (tripod). Be creative -- go high, go low, and remember, the camera doesn't have to pan and/or tilt in every shot. A series of locked down shots at different angles can be as interesting as a series of moving shots filmed from one point of view.

2x4-The Secret Weapon

Bolting the camera to a 2x4 can create some very dynamic angles by allowing the camera to be placed in positions that would not normally be accessible. It also permits the camera to be moved over, under and around objects, which can produce some very exciting action scenes. The ability to edit moving scenes with static scenes will enhance the production value of the finished piece.

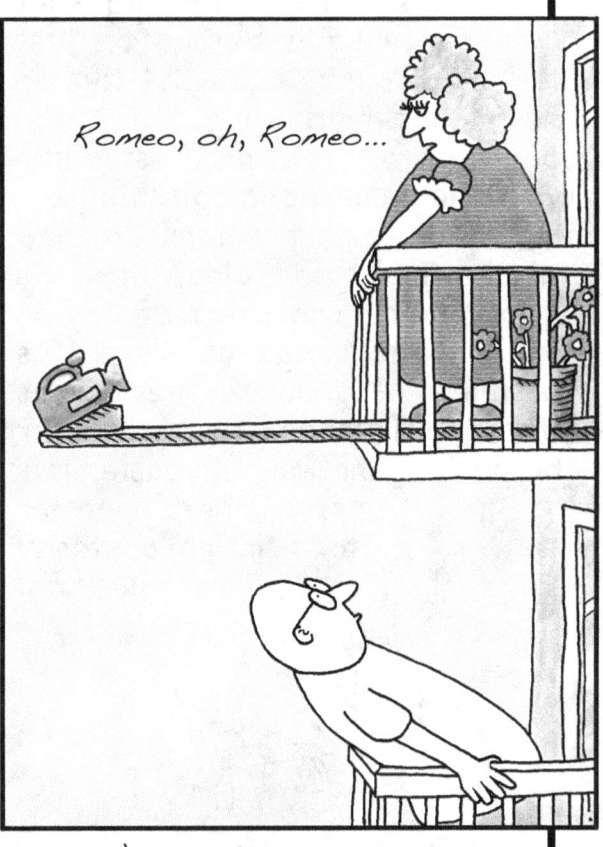

It's just Gladys filming one of her on-line dating videos.

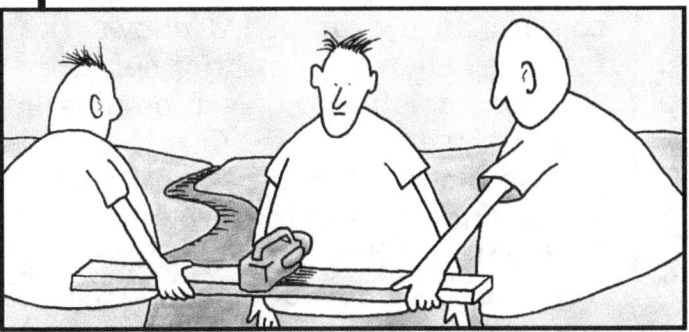

This is the money shot. Larry and I will be running with you and at the last moment we'll lift the camera over the car as it hits you.

Steady Boy..., Steady

Zooming out as wide as possible and turning on the camera's image stabilizer will help minimize any shaking that is generated by the motion of the camera. The tighter (closer) the lens is zoomed in on the subject, the shakier the image.

HELLO DOLLY

Anything with wheels can become a dolly -- a wheelchair, a cart, a hand truck. Dolly moves help create a smoother tracking shot when following a person or just moving through space. Utilizing the hand-held rig, position yourself for the most stability. With the camera's image stabilizer turned on, and the lens zoomed out as wide as possible, follow the action, being conscious of trying to keep the image as steady as possible. A good partner makes all the difference, the smoother the pushing motion, the easier it is for the camera operator to maintain a steady camera position.

LOW For a low angle on the fluid head, a hi-hat is required. It allows the camera to pan and tilt in a normal way very close to the ground.

LOWER To shoot a static low angle, set the camera on a box. Putting a sand bag on the box creates a soft surface to finesse the camera's final position.

LOWEST (Well, it can go lower-dig a hole.) The camera sitting on a sand bag or wedged up at ground level can produce a very dramatic shot.

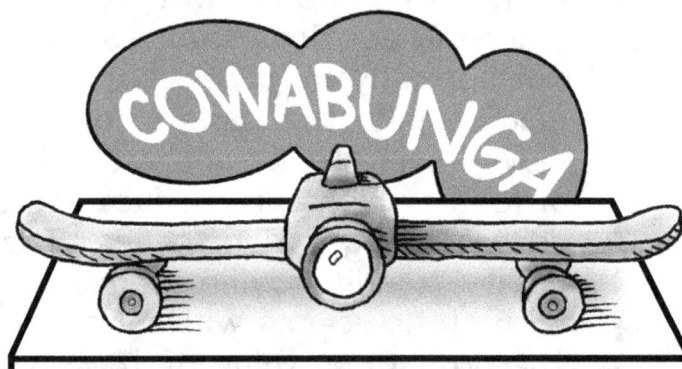

COWABUNGA

Moving shots give any project production value. Mounting the camera on a skateboard allows the camera to move on any flat surface--a floor, a table top, even outside if the surface is smooth. Create depth and drama in a scene by moving past something in the foreground (just in front of the camera) revealing the scene hidden behind it. Use a small wedge (rubber doorstop) to adjust the camera angle.

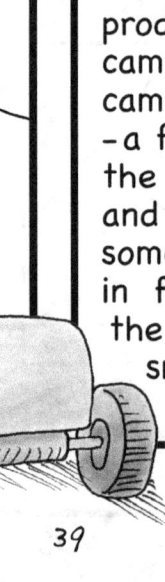

PROTECT THE LENS

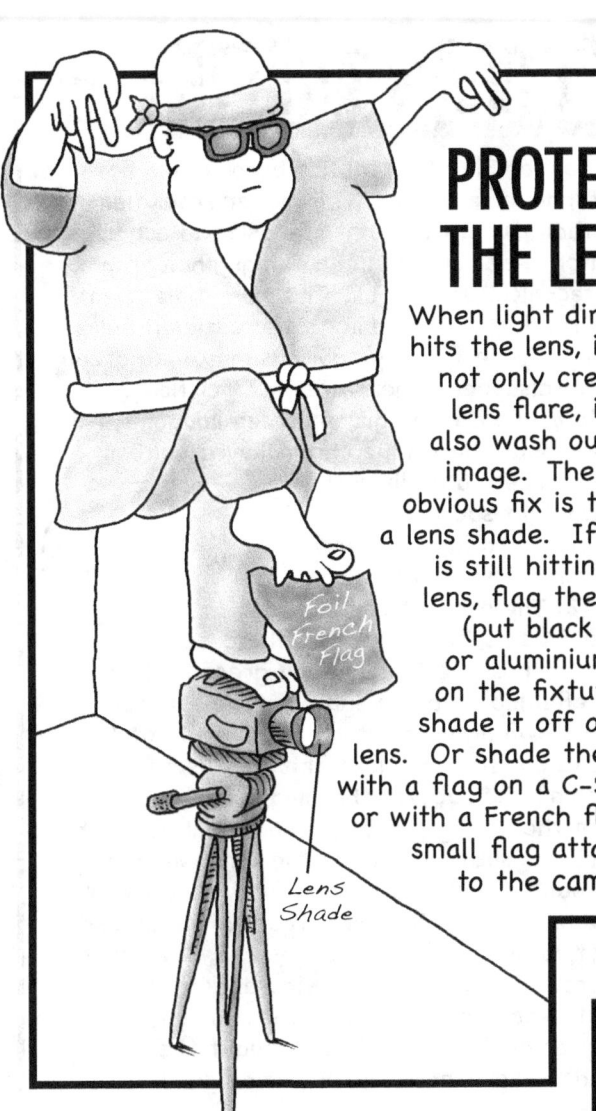

Foil French Flag

Lens Shade

When light directly hits the lens, it can not only create a lens flare, it can also wash out the image. The most obvious fix is to use a lens shade. If light is still hitting the lens, flag the light (put black wrap or aluminium foil on the fixture) to shade it off of the lens. Or shade the lens with a flag on a C-Stand or with a French flag (a small flag attached to the camera).

THE ZOOM IS A TOOL, NOT A CRUTCH.

Zooming in and out should only be used to check focus, or as an effect. Nothing makes a production look cheaper than seeing a bunch of zooms. Again, it calls attention to the camera and away from the story. Use the zoom to compose the shot, then pretend it's a prime (a fixed focus lens that can not zoom).

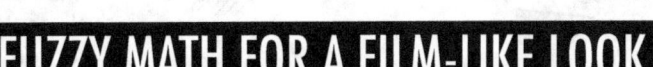

CIRCULAR POLARIZING FILTER

A great outside filter used to reduce reflections and glare on surfaces and improve contrast. It loses 1 to 2 f-stops, but does beautiful things to bright blue skies.

FUZZY MATH FOR A FILM-LIKE LOOK

1 The further the camera is away from the subject,

+2 and the further the subject is away from the background,

+3 with the camera zoomed in all the way on the subject and the f-stop at a low setting,

=4 the softer (out of focus) the background will appear-- creating a more film-like image.

extrapolating – The closer the camera is to the subject, and the wider the lens is zoomed out, the sharper (in focus) the background will appear.

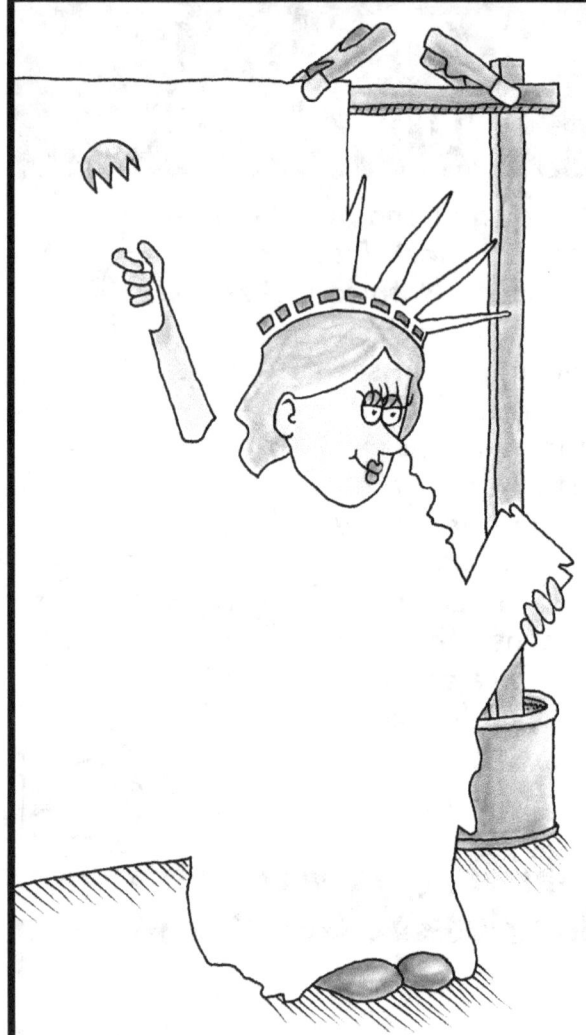

GREEN SCREEN

Green Screen (or Blue Screen) has become a very popular graphic effect. And with higher resolution High Definition cameras, it is much easier to achieve a clean chromakey. But, as in all things photographic, it has it's technical challenges. The more time spent setting up the key in the camera, the easier it will be in editing. Aside from the obvious, anything green (or blue) will disappear, there are three critical elements to attain a clean green screen image. **1.** The background should be a true chromakey green (or blue), and it needs to be lit evenly with its own light sources. The camera zebras or a light meter become a critical tool in this process. **2.** The subject being keyed should be as far away from the green background as possible to avoid any green spill that might be reflected onto the subject. The subject then gets its own lighting setup. Be careful not to cast shadows on the portion of the green screen directly behind the subject that might interfere with the key. In the keying process, if the tonal value of the edge of the subject is the same tonal value as the background it makes it harder for the keyer to find the edge. Backlighting will create a rim around the subject to help define the edges. **3.** The green screen exposure should be 1/2 f-stop darker than the subject exposure (example: subject at an f4, background at an f3.5). And, never light the subject and background with the same light source.

Hey, Dave..., I think I just figured out why they also make a blue screen.

SHOOT A SAFETY

Once a good take is in the can, if possible, it's always a good idea to shoot a backup just in case something happened that wasn't seen during the hero take. It's amazing how often the safety becomes the hero.

MAKEUP

It can make a huge difference when you are able to knock down the shine on someone's face. Assemble a small kit of powder and sponges (so you don't have to use the same disgusting sponge to apply more than one person's makeup). Don't overdo it--a light dusting of powder will usually do the trick; then just reapply when necessary.

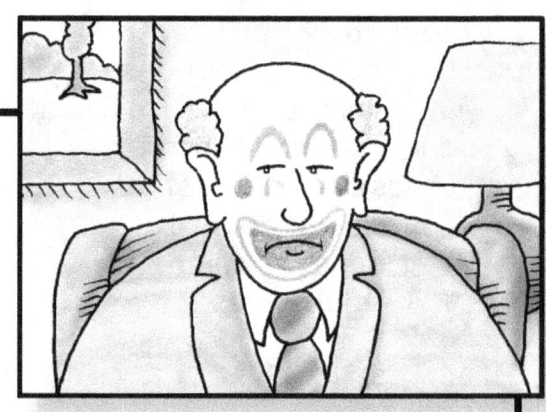

I came straight from work.

PICTURE THIS

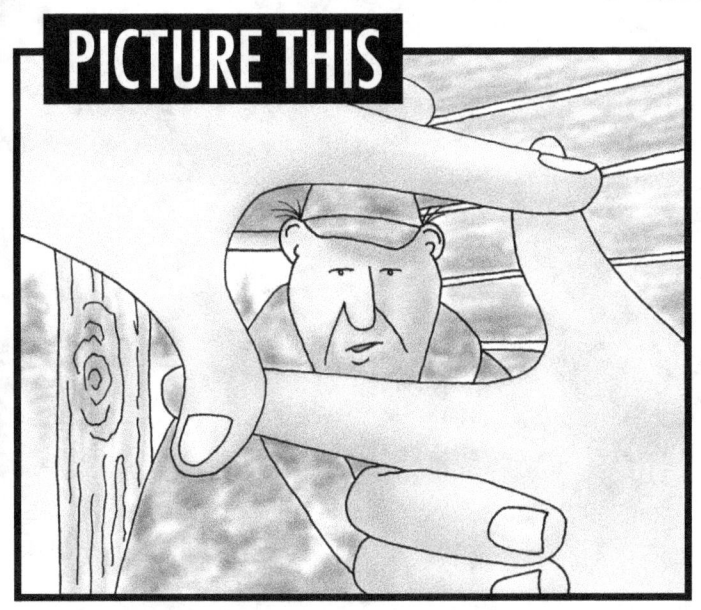

DID YOU SEE THAT?

When shooting, be aware that anything that moves in the frame will attract the attention of the viewer — people, traffic, sasquatch. Unless activity is part of the creative concept, find a location with minimal background movement. If there is no other choice, figure out a way to design the activity into the composition.

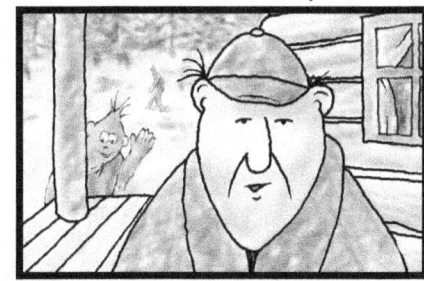

COMPOSITION...

Composition is fundamental to the shooting process. The way a scene is composed and shot adds an emotional element that can enhance the viewer's perception. The same way any erratic camera movement can become self-conscious and detract from the story, basic scene design can either draw you in or put you off.

DIRECTING THE EYE

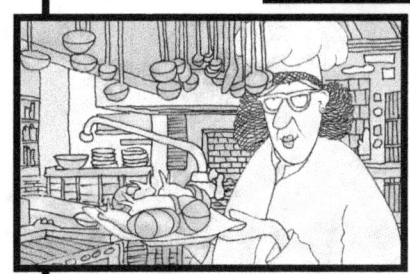
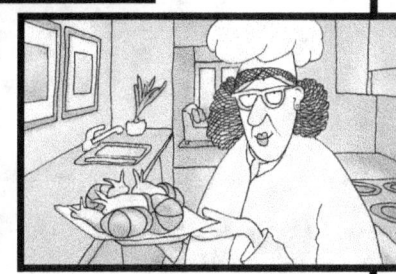

Cluttered Background   *Simple Background*

When composing a shot, backgrounds play a major role. The background should help focus attention to the subject, not compete for attention. Using depth of field, to throw the background out of focus, is a great way to direct the viewer's attention to what is in focus, the subject. If you're able to light the background, try techniques like a cookie (cookaloris) to create light and dark shapes.

THE RULE OF THIRDS

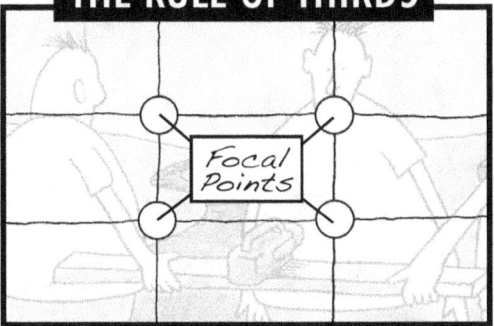

Focal Points

Seldom should anything you shoot be right in the middle of the frame. Create visual interest by shifting the focal point. Whether it's a person or a landscape, design the frame for the greatest visual impact. The "Rule of Thirds" is a great place to start.

LEARN TO SKETCH WITH THE CAMERA

To compose a shot you may have to move the camera — not only physically from one spot to another, but raise, lower, pan or tilt to find the position that gives you a well composed image.

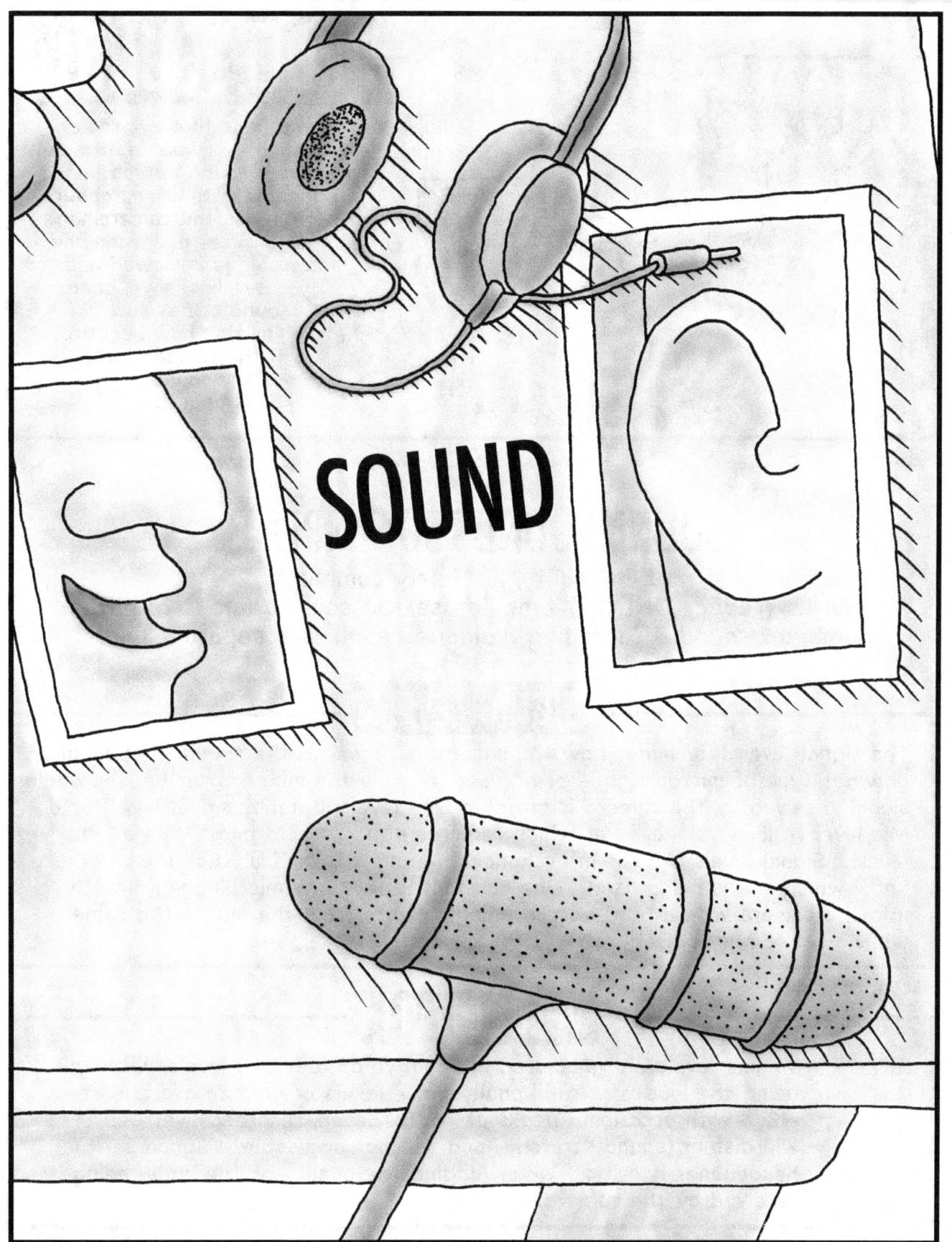

SOUND

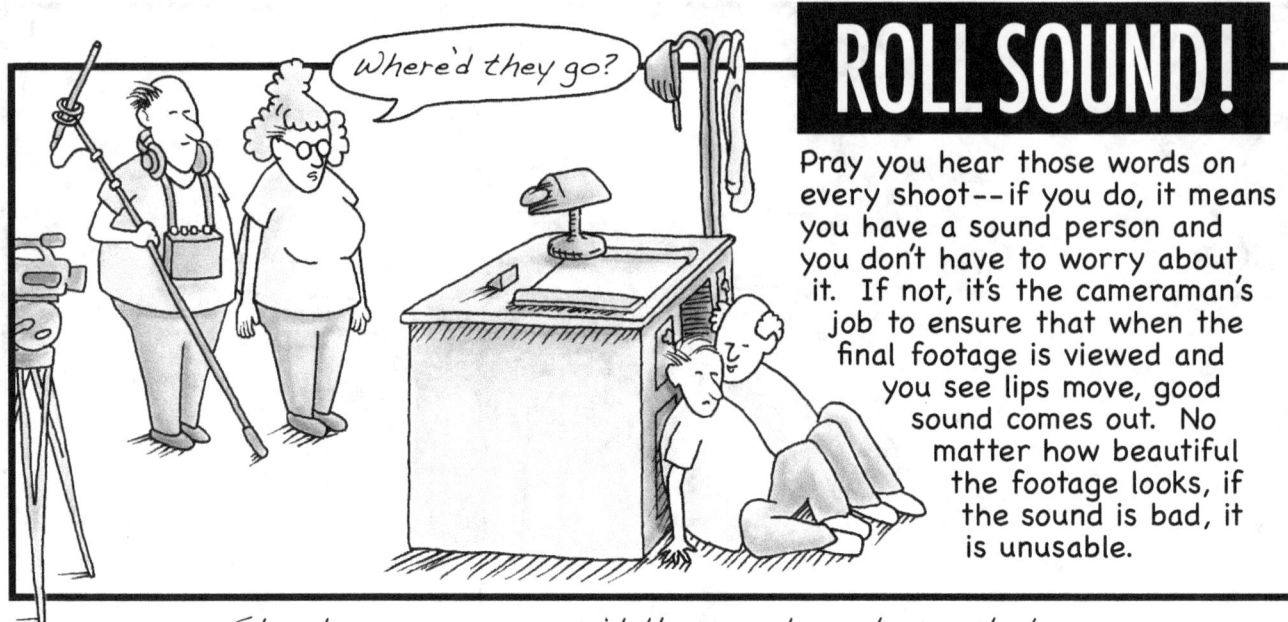

ROLL SOUND!

Pray you hear those words on every shoot--if you do, it means you have a sound person and you don't have to worry about it. If not, it's the cameraman's job to ensure that when the final footage is viewed and you see lips move, good sound comes out. No matter how beautiful the footage looks, if the sound is bad, it is unusable.

Stay down...someone said the sound guy has a shotgun.

SOUND SOUNDS SO SIMPLE.

But, in reality, it's fairly complex.
The ONLY (repeat, ONLY!!!) time to use the camera mic is to gather ambient sound. Recording dialogue requires a separate mic.

SIGNAL LEVELS

The signal level determines how the camera is receiving the sound. Depending on what type of microphone is being used, or how the mixer is set up, the audio signal received by the camera is either a Line level (a higher signal level) or a Mic level (a lower signal level which requires a pre amp to boost it to a Line level). Signal levels are not interchangeable and it is critical that the camera know which one is being used. One constant is that any mic plugged directly into the camera with a hard-wire running directly from the mic to the camera will be set to Mic level.

VOLUME LEVELS

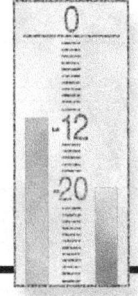

Volume levels are measured in negative dB (decibel) levels, with 0dB being the loudest. Traditionally, voice levels are set to average at -12dB with occasional peaks at -6dB. Levels recorded over 0dB will distort (sound scratchy) and will not be usable. A good set of headphones is critical when judging the quality of the audio being received by the camera.

SPLITTING HOT AND COLD

Most high-end cameras offer two audio channels. When using one microphone, a splitter can be used to send the same signal to both channel 1 and channel 2, allowing the volume for each channel to be set to a different level (hot on channel 1 at -12dB and cold on channel 2 at -20dB) to ensure if the hot channel blows out (distorts) the cold channel will still be usable.

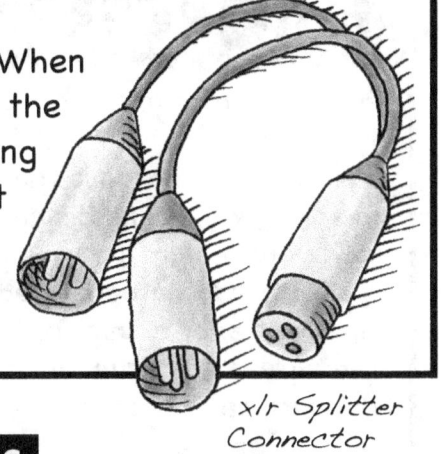

xlr Splitter Connector

TYPES OF MICROPHONES

Lavalier mic (aka Lav)

Hard-wire vs Wireless – A hard-wire refers to connecting the microphone directly to the camera or mixer via an xlr cable or mini plug. A wireless connection involves using a microphone connected to a transmitter, which then sends an audio signal to a receiver connected either directly to the camera or to a mixer that is connected to the camera.

Wireless Transmitter

Wireless Receiver

Lavalier Microphone – A Lav (or tie mic) is commonly used when the talent is moving or in a position that will not allow the Shotgun to be used because it will be seen (a wide shot). A Lav also helps eliminate background noise because it allows the mic to be placed closer to the source.

Shotgun Microphone

A shotgun mic with a windscreen on a boom pole.

A Shotgun is the mic most people associate with sound recording. It's a directional mic (point it at the noise) attached to the end a boom pole. Commonly there will be a person holding the boom pole to point it at the talent.

Both is Best – Using a Shotgun in combination with a Lav is the optimum setup for audio, and offers a good mix of levels and aesthetics. With the Lav on one channel and the Shotgun on the second channel, it is possible to mix them in post to make one mic more prominent than the other, or even eliminate one mic completely.

A Mixer – A mixer is an interface to control multiple microphones. Mixers come in various configurations from two channels to many channels. Field mixers usually have three or four channels (three or four mics) that are mixed into one or two channels and then fed to the camera via a hard-wire or wirelessly. A mixer can output a Mic level or a Line level signal.

MIC PLACEMENT

Placement of a microphone is critical. Typically, a Lav is placed 6" to 12" from the mouth. A mic that is too far away will sound distant no matter how high the volume level is set. Lavs can be clipped to a lapel, a tie, or a shirt collar. The wire is then run under the garment where it will not be seen. If the talent is speaking predominately to one side, the mic should be placed on that side.

Here

Or Here

Hiding the mic

Tape folded in a triangle (sticky side out) and tape over the top.

A Lav can be hidden under a coat, a shirt or a collar by taping it in a variety of ways. It can even be taped to the skin. 'Clothes Rustle' can cause one of the biggest problems with a hidden mic. If it happens, try another spot.

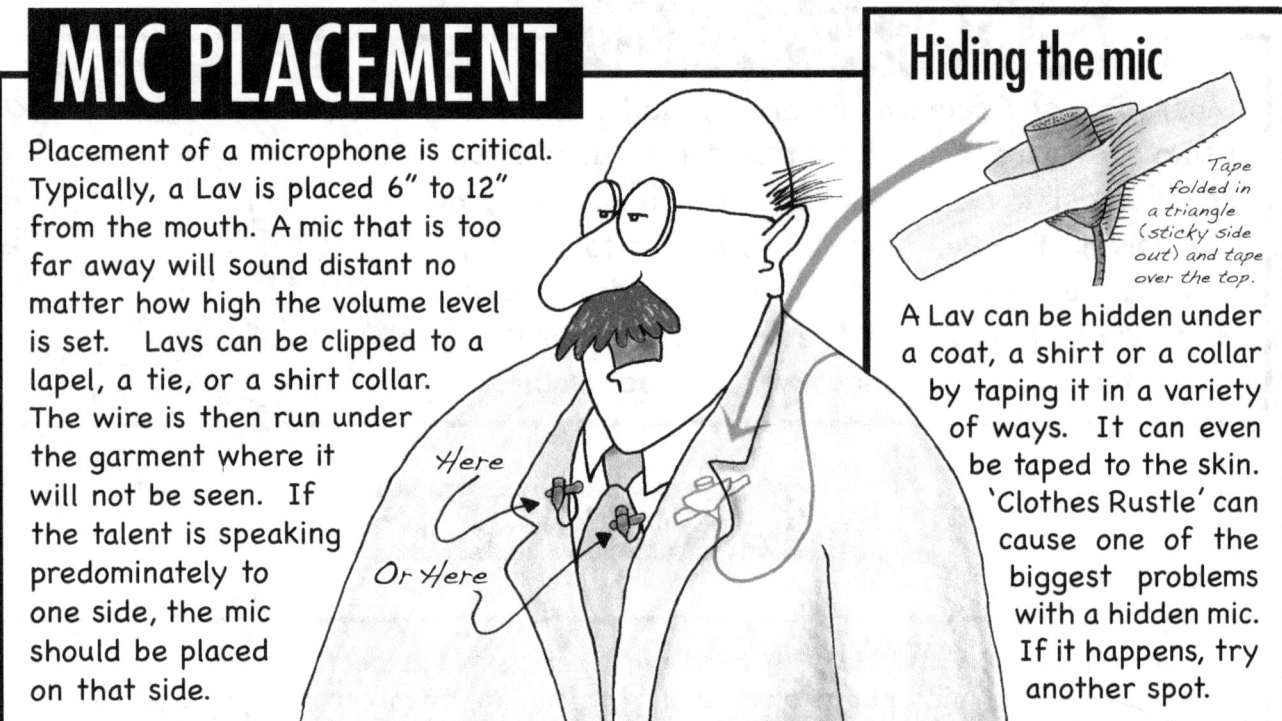

When a power cable runs parallel to an audio cable it creates quite a... **BZZZZZZZZZZZ** ...to eliminate the buzz, run them perpendicular (at 90°).

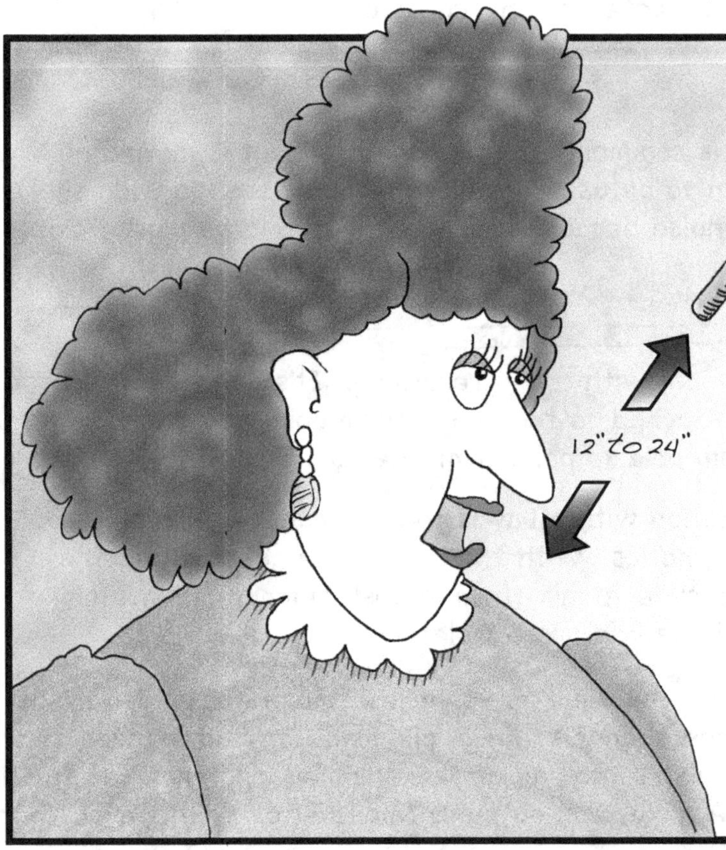

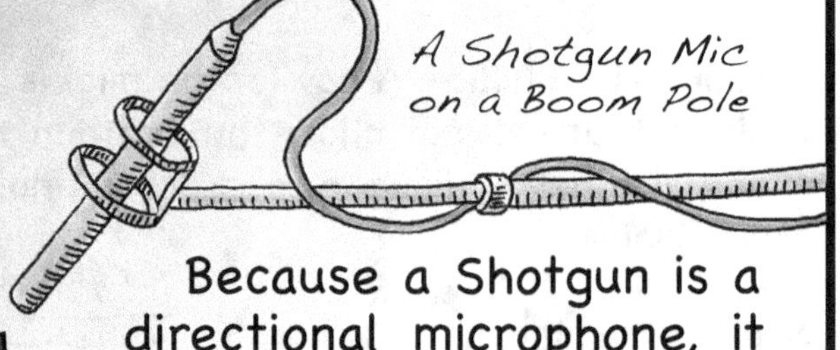

A Shotgun Mic on a Boom Pole

12" to 24"

Because a Shotgun is a directional microphone, it is crucial for it to be pointed directly at the audio source it is expected to record. If the source is moving, the mic needs to move with the source in order to maintain the audio quality. It is a great way to gather multiple audio setups quickly when there is no time to attach and remove a Lav.

HEADPHONES

Monitoring the audio signal at the camera as it is recorded will ensure the sound being captured is as pure as it can be. If a mixer is being used, the audio should still be monitored at the camera to make certain a clean signal is actually getting to the camera. Monitoring the audio at the mixer only confirms that the signal is being received by the mixer.

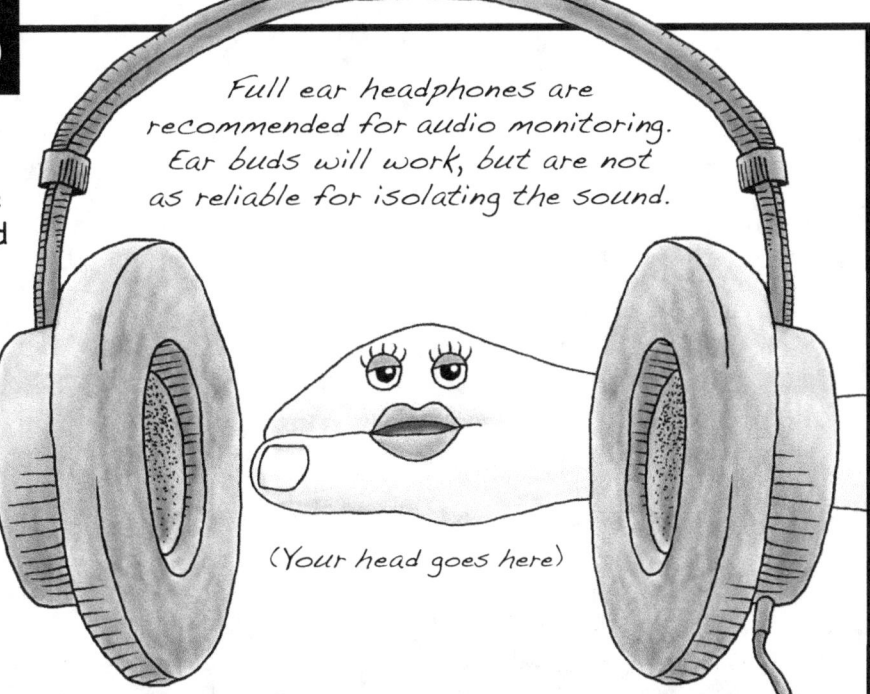

Full ear headphones are recommended for audio monitoring. Ear buds will work, but are not as reliable for isolating the sound.

(Your head goes here)

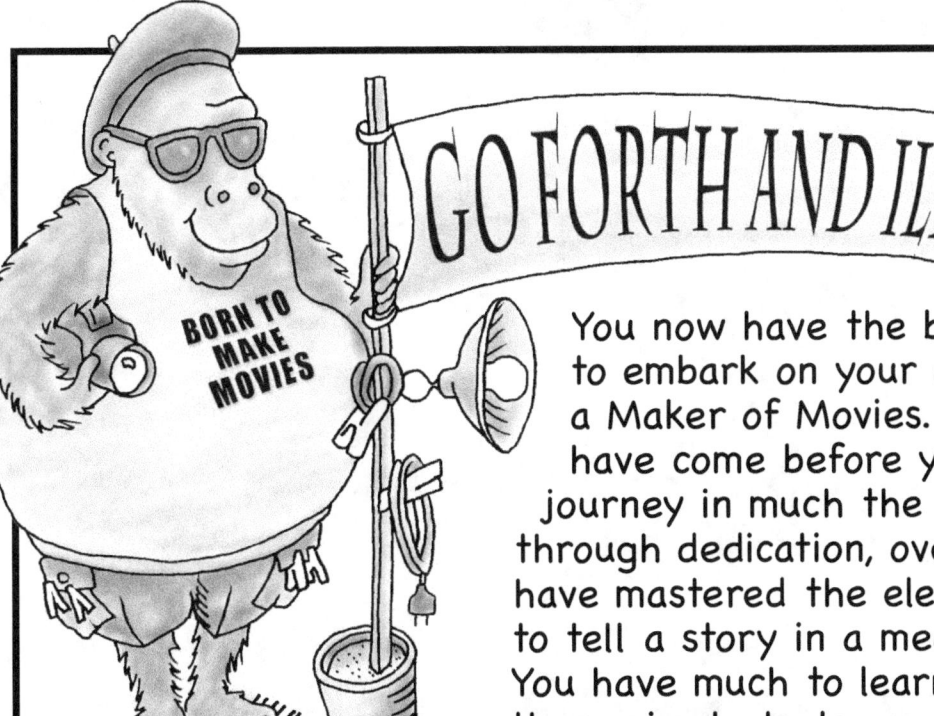

BORN TO MAKE MOVIES

GO FORTH AND ILLUMINATE

You now have the basic knowledge to embark on your adventure as a Maker of Movies. Those who have come before you began their journey in much the same way. And through dedication, over time they have mastered the elements required to tell a story in a meaningful way. You have much to learn, but with these simple tools, your ability to make artistic films is only limited by the scope of your imagination, not the size of your wallet. So, what are you waiting for? Somewhere out there a work light is calling your name. Go make a movie.

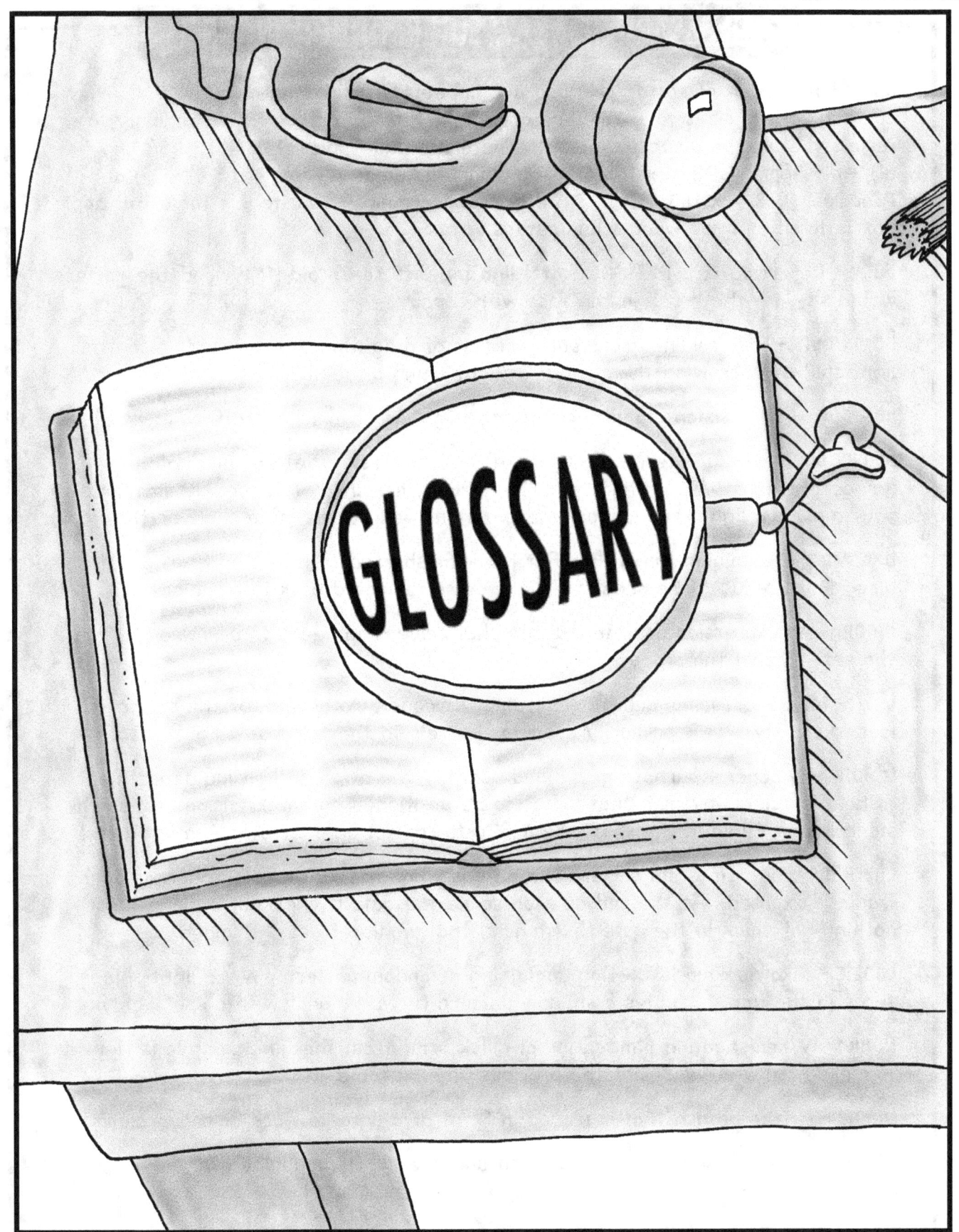

A GLOSSARY OF A FEW FUN PRODUCTION TERMS

Apple Box – Made of sturdy plywood and capable of holding a lot of weight. They come in various sizes to enable the grip department to stack them randomly to raise something to a specific height. There are Full Apples (19 3/4' x 11 3/4' x 8'), Half Apples (19 3/4' x 11 3/4' x 4'), Quarter Apples (19 3/4' x 11 3/4' x 2') and Pancakes (19 3/4' x 11 3/4' x 1'). The grip department's favorite use for a full apple box is to sit on it between scene setups.

Baby – Referring to a 1K (1000 watt) lighting fixture. In old Hollywood the gaffers would say "Hit the broad in the face with a baby."

Barn Doors – Four folding doors on the front of a lighting fixture used to control light spill by narrowing the amount of light being projected.

Best Boy – The assistant to either the chief lighting technician (gaffer), or key grip.

Beaver Board – (aka Pigeon on a Pancake) The smallest variety of an apple box (pancake) with a 5/8" lighting spud (Baby Plate) attached with screws. It allows you to place a light very low or where a stand will not fit (on a shelf or the floor).

Blackwrap – Aluminum foil with a flat black finish used to flag a light. The flat black finish reduces the danger of light being reflected back into the scene.

Broom – An expression used to indicate that something needs to be removed from the set. "Broom the product."

C-47 – (aka Peg, Ammo, Bullet) An ordinary wooden clothespin (of the spring-loaded variety). It is primarily used to clip gels to the front of a light.

C-Stand – A general purpose grip stand used by the grip and lighting department to hold virtually anything that needs to be positioned on an extension arm so the stand is not visible in the shot (like a flag to control light, or even the light itself).

Check the Gate – In a film camera the gate is what the film runs through as each frame is exposed. At the end of each scene the gate is checked to make sure nothing got stuck in the gate (like a hair) that would effect the image.

Cookie – (aka Cookaloris) A flag containing a random pattern. When light shines through the flag it creates a shadow pattern (it works best with a spot light).

Dailies – When shooting film, an initial quick print from the film negative is viewed to make sure what was shot the previous day is usable.

Dingle – A tree branch that is placed in front of a light to work as a cookaloris.

Dirt – A sandbag used to secure a stand and keep it from tipping over. "Throw some dirt on that C-Stand."

Doorway Dolly – A sturdy plywood dolly designed to fit through a doorway. It is used to carry a camera on a tripod, or to just transport equipment.

Dutch Angle – Tilting the camera at an angle that is not level with the horizon.

Flags – Metal frames, in an array of sizes, holding opaque or transparent material. The frame is then secured on a C-Stand by the grip department to control light.

Flood It – The term used when focusing a light with a fresnel (a glass lens) to a wide beam. When wanting to focus it to a narrow beam, the term is to spot it.

Gaffer – The chief lighting technician in charge of the electrical department and responsible for the design of the lighting plan for a given project.

Gobo – The gripping head of a C-Stand used to hold equipment.

Key Grip – Person working with the chief lighting technician setting flags to create shadow effects. Also supervises dollies, and any mechanical apparatus or special rigging required by the Director of Photography.

Key Light – The primary light source illuminating a subject.

Kicker – A backlight used to create a rim highlight to separate the subject from the background (aka "Hair Light"). "Whack him with a kicker."

Mickey – (aka "Redhead") An open face (it has no focusing lens) 1K light.

M.O.S. – Early film jargon for no sound--"Mit Out Sound."

NTSC and ATSC– NTSC (National Television System Committee) is the old broadcast standard for North America. 525-line/60Hz (480i), 30fps (frames per second). ATSC (Advanced Television System Committee) is the new high definition digital format for wide screen 16:9 images up to 1920x1080 pixels. Footage can be shot at a variety of frame rates (30fps, 60fps, 24fps).

PAL – (Phase Alternate Line) the broadcast standard for many countries outside of the U.S. 625-line/50Hz (576i), 25/50 frames per second.

Shiny Board – A reflector used to aim sunlight as a lighting source (Key, Back or Fill).

Soft – An image that appears out of focus is said to be soft. "He looks soft." Images that are in focus are referred to as sharp.

Stinger – An extension cord, usually with a three pronged grounded plug.

Strike – Break down a camera setup for a move to the next setup. "Strike the set."

Wrap – Filming is finished--it is time to strike the set and go home. "It's a wrap!"

NOTES

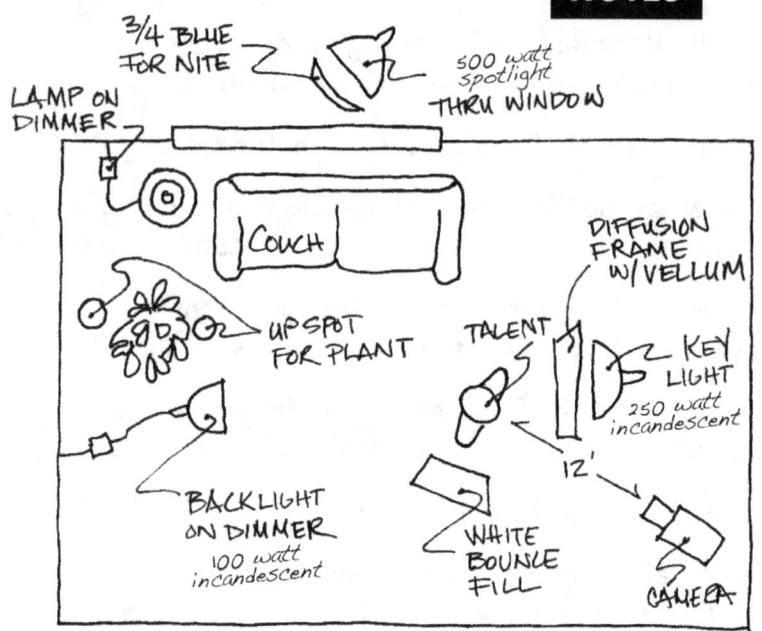

3/4 BLUE FOR NITE

500 watt spotlight
THRU WINDOW

LAMP ON DIMMER

COUCH

DIFFUSION FRAME W/VELLUM

UP SPOT FOR PLANT

TALENT

KEY LIGHT
250 watt incandescent

12'

BACKLIGHT ON DIMMER
100 watt incandescent

WHITE BOUNCE FILL

CAMERA

Camera F-stop 2.8

Keep notes on how a scene is lit. Then when you compare it to the final shot, you will have a good reference tool for determining which lighting techniques work well.

NOTES

www.ingramcontent.com/pod-product-compliance
Lightning Source LLC
Chambersburg PA
CBHW081257180526
45170CB00007B/2471